SUCCESSFUL STRATEGIES FOR REAL ESTATE AGENTS

SUCCESSFUL STRATEGIES FOR REAL ESTATE AGENTS

A Step-By-Step System on How to Succeed In Today's Real Estate World

Floyd Wickman

Executive Press

High Point, North Carolina

Library of Congress Catalog Card Number: 86-82782

ISBN 0-9399-7501-7

Published by Executive Press
806 Westchester Drive
High Point, NC   27262

Printed in the United States of America
10 9 8 7 6 5 4 3

I would like to dedicate this book to Mike Ferry for his belief in me and for all his help.

Contents

Preface

The road to hell is paved with good intentions, because good intentions alone will take a person nowhere fast!

One hundred percent of the people who go into the real estate business every year have very high intentions. And it's easy to see why. Selling real estate is a lucrative profession that offers high rewards for those agents who know what they're doing.

Unfortunately, not every agent is good at it. In fact, something happens to seventy percent of all real estate agents during their first year in the business.

They quit.

Oh, they don't always leave right away. Sometimes, they hang around for a while. In fact, I've seen people in a state of "quit" for two years before they finally clean out their desk and walk out the door.

Why did they leave? Perhaps they felt they didn't have the talent. Maybe they were inhibited because they thought they didn't have the natural gift of gab that successful agents seem to possess. They could have believed their careers didn't take off because they lacked the connections that multi-million-dollar producers seem to have.

For whatever reason, they decided real estate just wasn't for them. And the shame of it is, it could have been. I've been in this business since 1967, and I've never met a person who didn't have all the basic ingredients to be a successful real estate agent.

There's nothing special about "special" people in real estate. You don't have to have an exceptionally high I.Q., or be the best looking person in town, or be loaded with natural charisma. True, none of these attributes will hurt, and neither will hard work, although even that alone won't guarantee your success. Some of the hardest working agents I've ever known drew poverty-level incomes because they didn't work smart. To make it in this business, an agent must learn to work smart. And that is done only by knowing the techniques.

Anyone in any profession must know techniques to survive. Should a funeral director watching over a $15,000 service be happy? What salesperson wouldn't be happy about a transaction that's anywhere from three to five times the norm? But should the director smile throughout the service? Of course not. That would be most inappropriate. So instead, the director must look somber, if not outright sad. Now that's knowing the techniques!

Fortunately, real estate agents don't have to keep such tight rein on their emotions, although they do need to develop and be able to present occasionally what is known as a "poker face."

IT'S IN THE CARDS

Have you ever known an agent who seemed to be shot full of luck? No matter what happened, the agent would pull down listing after listing, sale after sale? Everybody knows someone like that. The basic truth is, one out of every ten real estate agents is going to make it in this business, no matter what. It's just in the cards.

Several years ago, I was running a recruiting ad for an office in Pleasant Ridge, Michigan, when a fellow named Domonico Siciliano walked in and applied for a job. It only took me about ten seconds to decide that there was no way on earth I was going to hire him. It wasn't that I didn't like the way he was dressed, although I didn't like his appearance. It wasn't that I didn't like his overbearing approach, although that didn't appeal to me, either.

The reason that I didn't hire Domonico Siciliano was quite simple: To sell real estate in the United States, it helps to know the English language, and Domonico had never taken the trouble to learn it. Besides, we also didn't have any training manuals printed in Italian.

But what Domonico lacked in familiarity with our language, he made up with persistence. He kept hounding me for a job. I used every technique I could think of to get rid of him, but he kept coming back. Finally, I did what any chicken broker would have done. I hired him.

After signing his application, I said, "Domonico, you go to school and study hard. And if you pass, give me a call." I really thought that would take care of him. But I had forgotten about his persistence. So when the telephone rang several months later, I was quite surprised—and unnerved—to hear Domonico.

"Allo, Meester Floyd. Thees ees Domonico. I no pass-a the test-a."

"Oh," I said, stifling a relieved chuckle. "I'm awfully sorry. That's too bad."

"Yes, that's-a right." Domonico agreed. "It is too bad-a. But for you, Meester Floyd. I keep-a trying."

He would. But what the heck? There will be ice cream parlors in hell before he passes the exam, I thought. So I relaxed, wished him good luck and told him to keep in touch. Then I forgot about him.

Domonico took the test a second time. He failed. He took it a third time and failed again. In the state of Michigan, three strikes and you're out. The only way you can take the real estate certification exam a fourth time is to either be handicapped, which Domonico wasn't, or by getting special permission from the state board, which Domonico did.

On his fourth and final try, he scored a seventy-five. That's barely passing. But in terms of certification, it's just as good as one hundred. Domonico got his license, and I had to keep my word by hiring him.

And after his first year in the business, he had closed ninety-four transactions! That's like a one-man office. I've seen office staffs with a dozen or more agents that didn't generate that much business. Yet, this guy, who spoke broken English at best, set all kinds of records, all by himself.

Yet this agent wouldn't know a technique if it bit him on the ankle. Domonico ruined so many of my new people because he was a natural. I couldn't discuss techniques with a trainee while Domonico was setting the woods on fire every day, using his own, unorthodox, unapproved, against-the-book methods.

But Domonico was in that ten percent of real estate agents who can make it with their eyes closed. They have the gift of gab, the natural charisma, the willingness to work, the connections, the background . . . whatever it takes to rise in the industry.

This book wasn't written for that ten percent (although even they might pick up a few pointers from it). This book is for the ninety percent of real estate agents who must rely on techniques to survive.

THIS BOOK IS FOR YOU

This includes the beginning real estate agent who needs a helpful push into the business. It also includes the agent who has been in the business for a while but wants to get a fresh start by going back to the basics. It also includes the successful but overworked agent who wants to become more productive and efficient. Twelve-hour days, six and seven days per week is no way to make a living.

I promise you, if you learn the techniques—not merely memorize them—and put them to work, you'll do more than just survive! You not only will be within the thirty percent range of real estate agents who stay in the business, but you'll also have the potential to reach that very small percentage responsible for the majority of real estate sales.

This is not hype. The principles in this book have been tested throughout North America in my "Sweathogs" real estate agent-training program. In more than thirty states and all Canadian provinces, I've taught thousands of agents these same principles I'm offering here, and they have attained some impressive results.

On an average, my "Sweathogs" chalked up eight listings and five sales each in an eighty-four day period. Their take-home earnings increased by about two hundred percent per person, and they did an average dollar volume of $910,000.

The real estate business is the same anywhere in North America. I've covered enough ground and worked with enough agents to know. And I've learned that if something works over and over in every part of the continent, then it indeed works! You don't have to reinvent the wheel.

Unless you're like Domonico Siciliano, being successful in the real estate business is going to take a combination of techniques and application. So to stay in the business, you must learn the technology that works. It's all here. The techniques have worked for me, and they have worked for my more than four thousand graduate real estate agents throughout the United States and Canada.

If you're really serious about selling real estate, they will work for you.

This book will show you how to find prospects, prepare successful listings, separate lookers from buyers and how to make buyers feel good about signing on the dotted line. And considering the price of real estate (not to mention the ensuing commissions), that knowledge alone should be worth many times the price of the book.

But you'll also learn how to make the most of your property demonstrations, how to develop showmanship, what to watch for in prospective buyers and how to react to them. And finally, you will learn to cut through prospects' stalls and to identify and handle their objections, so you can make the sale.

That's the bottom line, isn't it? Because if we don't make the sale, the bills don't get paid.

DON'T GET OUT! GET IN

If your commissions aren't paying your bills, don't get out of the real estate business. Get into it! This book will give you all you need to know to keep your finances in the black from now on. Read this book once for information, twice to establish familiarity and a third time for strength.

Then keep it for future reference, because I'll guarantee you that if you take to heart the principles offered, you'll never consider leaving the real estate business again.

I believe in what I'm saying, because I became a multi-million-dollar producer using these same principles. And take my word for it: When I entered the real estate business almost two decades ago, there was no one alive who knew less about salesmanship, techniques and working with people than I did.

If you have the mentality to pass the state licensing exam, you've got the potential to become a multi-million-dollar producer. If you don't believe me, ask one of my thousands of "Sweathogs."

Better yet, read this book and decide for yourself.

Section 1

GETTING THE RIGHT START

1

Lay Your Foundations

While conducting a training session once, I met an agent named Larry. He was quite a sight. Sad little fellow, he was. His whole demeanor figuratively screamed melancholy.

"You just can't sell real estate in this economy," Larry said.

"Ah, come on, Larry," I said. "Be positive."

"I am positive," Larry shot back. "You just can't sell real estate in this economy."

I doubt seriously that Larry persuaded any multi-million-dollar producers that selling real estate was impossible. But one thing is for certain: He convinced himself, and that made all the difference in the world between his being a success and a failure.

People like Larry are not uncommon, unfortunately. You've probably known a few yourself. They are always looking for someone or something to blame for their poor performances. And they automatically expect poor performances because they have successfully convinced themselves they can't do any better.

Then there are positive souls who know that adversity breeds real success, that every problem has a solution, and that finding it not only will make them better salespeople, but better human beings as well.

Every person in the world is destined for success—even if it means succeeding at being a failure. You could be like Larry and give up. But, by reading this book, you're obviously interested in success, and how to attain it.

As they say, if life gives you lemons, make lemonade. History is filled with great people whose beginnings were bleak, indeed. Take the case of a poor little boy who grew up in a British orphanage. He was able to emigrate to America in the early 1900s, but he had little or no money when he arrived.

But he had a dream and a desire. And with his own creative ingenuity, along with steady doses of hard work, he became a multi-millionaire through the magic of movies. He eventually produced, directed, wrote, scored and starred in his own full-length motion pictures that packed theater houses around the world!

No one can see the familiar derby, oversized shoes, baggy pants, small coat and cane without thinking of Charlie Chaplin. He took his knowledge of being poor and converted it into the "little tramp" who entertained theater-goers for decades.

Talk about lemonade! Maybe you won't be able to make quite that kind of impact in the real estate business. But you never know.

WHAT'S YOUR ATTITUDE?

It's a matter of mental attitudes—positive and logical. It takes both. Agents can be as positive as they will, but without logic, they'll hit bottom fast.

It's like the fellow who convinced himself he could fly without an airplane. To prove it, he jumped off the top of a fifteen-story building. Did he fly? Of course not. But a sixth-floor office worker heard him shout on his way down, "So far, so good!"

Granted, that's positive, but hardly logical.

On the other hand, logic without enthusiasm is like this book itself. It has all agents need to know to sell real estate, but it's not going to sell it for them. Only they can do that, and the first step is believing they can.

Let me repeat: There is nothing special about "special" people in the real estate business. It's what they do every day that counts. Aside from the Domonico Sicilianos of the world (the persistent agent I mentioned in the preface), the people who succeed in this business are those who learn the techniques and how to apply them. And successful agents refuse to be controlled by prospects. Instead, they know how to take control of a situation without necessarily manipulating the participants.

Multi-million-dollar producers in the real estate business don't allow themselves to be manipulated by unqualified buyers and unreasonable sellers. A successful agent won't take a listing (real estate terminology for an exclusive agreement authorizing a particular agent to sell a home) from a homeowner who sets a price that is twenty-five percent higher than market value. Why? Because the odds of ever getting the commission from the sale is slim, because no one is likely to buy the house at such an inflated price.

An agent who knows the business won't be caught demonstrating a home to a prospect who can't afford to buy. Why? Because if the prospect can't buy the home, why waste the time showing it? This is time that could be spent showing the home to a prospect who could afford it and, possibly, who very well might buy.

Real estate business practices might be different if agents earned straight salaries. But this isn't the case. Agents are paid only if people buy from them, or if the houses they list are sold, either by them or other agents. So agents are directly responsible for the amount of their incomes and must be in control of all business situations. When they go on listing appointments (meetings to convince homeowners to allow them to handle the sales), they go with positive attitudes. They don't just "see" if they can get the listings. They "see" if they want them. Time is money, and successful agents simply cannot afford to waste it.

IT'S NO FAIRY TALE

All this may sound like a fairy tale about the little steam engine that couldn't climb the steep hill because it didn't think it was able. Yet, it finally did, once it convinced itself that it could.

But life is no fairy tale, and all this psychology won't really work for you, right?

Wrong. It will work, if you just believe it. Of course, it takes more than just believing in yourself. The positive and logical attitudes are just the initial steps. There are other principles that successful agents must master.

DEVELOP AN INVENTORY

The amount of money an agent will make in the real estate business is in direct proportion to the number of listings with his or her name on them. That means that the agent must develop a substantial inventory of homes to be sold by getting the listings for them.

This is a process called prospecting, and here's an exercise that will teach the basic principle behind it. First, take three sheets of paper. On the first, list the names of everyone with whom you've ever done business. On the second, list the names of your friends and relatives. On the third, list the names of everyone else you know in your town or city.

Then throw those three pages away, because if you try to sell real estate only to people you know, you'll starve.

THE TELEPHONE: THE DREADED ALLY?

There are several good ways to get prospects, and chapter three will cover them. But the best advice I can give from the beginning is to get comfortable with the telephone.

Do you mind calling total strangers, just to ask them if they or anybody they know are thinking about selling their houses? I hope not, because that's the best way to get started or re-started in this business.

Whenever I explain this principle in my training seminars, I'll always get a question from some agent like poor Larry who will ask, "Floyd, isn't that called (gulp) cold canvassing?" And he'll stand there, almost trembling, with a look on his face that makes me wonder how he got into this business at all.

No matter what a person does for a living, any tool that can positively affect sales and/or earnings shouldn't be feared. It should be welcomed with open arms. And that's what the telephone is to real estate agents—a tool that can make the difference between poverty and a six-figure income.

Listings are indeed the name of the game. The basic principle of any business is inventory control, and multi-million-dollar producers know that the real money is made by building and maintaining a certain number of listings.

Sure, agents get commissions for their sales. But anybody can sell a home. Some agents sell homes in spite of themselves. That's because houses sell themselves. An agent can't sell a house to someone who doesn't want it.

In any given area, a certain number of homes are going to be sold next month, regardless of how many agents are at work. Successful real estate agents can stay successful only by controlling as much of the inventory as possible.

But it's not easy. It takes work. To be successful, agents must accept the fact that, at some point in their careers, they must work to build their inventories. Agents may do this for the right reasons— that is, to earn a lot of money and build a secure future for themselves. Or they may wait until they get one of those "four-word motivational talks" from their brokers: "You've got thirty days!"

The telephone is the best method of prospecting available. Yet, I've known agents who say, "I'd rather starve than use the telephone." And they starve, all right. I've also known some agents who say, "I'd rather prospect by going door-to-door." That's fine, except for two reasons:

1. An agent can canvass more residences in less time via telephone than by going from door to door.

2. Door-to-door prospecting is a great public relations tactic to build future business (which I'll thoroughly discuss later). But right now, the new agent is more concerned with paying this month's bills.

To lay the foundation for success, agents should get a cross-reference book (city directory) and start calling residences until they find someone who is thinking about selling a home. Sure, most calls won't turn up anything. But just a few leads can result in enough commissions to pay a lot of bills.

LEARN TO SELL

Here's another piece of sage advice: Know how to sell.

Now don't slam the book shut and throw it across the room. You may be thinking, "What kind of idiot does this man Wickman think I am? Of course I have to know how to sell to succeed in real estate."

But do you know how much selling it takes to reach the point when you can say, "Okay, Mr. Buyer, here's the pen. I'll need your okay on this. And press hard, this is cheap carbon"?

First, agents must sell to the seller. Just because a seller is thinking about selling doesn't automatically mean the agent will get the listing. Sometimes, the agent must "sell" sellers on listing. Sometimes, the agent must "sell" them on listing now, at a particular price, with specific terms, at a certain commission, for a particular length of time.

Then agents must sell to the buyer. Just because a buyer is looking for a home doesn't mean he or she is going to let a particular agent find it. And when "the right house" is found, then the agent may have to "sell" the seller on accepting an offer lower than the asking price. And when the seller instead suggests a counter-offer, the agent must go back and "sell" the buyer on the practicality of compromise.

That's a lot of selling! In fact, selling is ninety percent of this business. Real estate is only the product. An agent can know virtually nothing about real estate and still succeed, as long as he or she knows how to sell. On the other hand, agents who know everything about real estate will be in big trouble if they don't know how to sell.

It's very important to become adept at selling. Real estate agents go to licensing school and study the profession for weeks. They graduate with a thorough knowledge of real estate. But eighty percent of them don't know how to sell. And that's most unfortunate, because they're either going to have to learn, or they'll eventually drop, or starve, out of the business.

If you know how to sell, there's no reason you can't be among the top twenty percent of real estate agents.

SELL YOURSELF

Just remember that people don't care how much you know, unless they know how much you care. All the knowledge in the world won't help you unless your prospects think you're all right.

Agents who show concern for sellers will improve significantly their chances of getting listings. Agents who show concern for buyers will improve significantly their chances of getting commissions.

So agents should learn to show concern, yet keep control of the situation. And there is no better way to do that than by asking questions.

QUESTIONS GET RESULTS

There is power in questions! The person asking is in control, and the person answering is most interested. And the more interested prospects are, the better the odds an agent will wind up doing business with them.

When talking with a prospect, ask the right questions. I call them "wopen" questions. That's nothing more than an open question that starts with the five "Ws"—who, what, when, where and why.

Think about it. A question started with one of those words will get more than a simple "yes" or "no" answer. Prospects must elaborate, and this will bring all kinds of valuable information agents may use to serve them.

For example, let's start with the question, "Where do you want to move?" The answer could be as varied as there are places in the world. Then you ask, "Why do you want to move?" The possibilities are endless. "When do you want to move?" Now the agent is getting more specific. "What kind of a house do you want?" The agent is learning about the desired number of rooms, design, square footage, price range and area. Just look at what those four questions can tell.

Agents also should know how to ask other questions that take a bit more nerve. For example, "What would it take for you to list with me tonight, Mr. and Mrs. Seller?" Or, "Wouldn't you like to buy this house today, Mr. and Mrs. Buyer?"

Agents must have courage in this business. Most of the time, they must ask for the listing or the sale. Prospects won't always offer. Agents who don't ask for business can be sure that there are enough competitors who will ask. And many times, they'll get it, all because they asked for it.

Remember, the more nerve you have, the more money you will earn.

PUT SHOWMANSHIP TO WORK

Have you ever seen television advertisements for certain unusual (for lack of a better word) products such as a jar-and-glass cutter or a pocket-sized fishing rod? They're a lot like the commercials for three-album record collections of a bygone era's "Top 40" hits.

They're all the same. The video portion includes demonstrations of the devices or display of the attractively designed record jackets. And the audio portion features an announcer who talks six hundred words per minute, rapidly extolling the virtues of the products and creating an impression that people who don't act fast will die and go to hell!

These products must attract a lot of buyers, because television stations literally litter the air waves with them. And one reason these products are so popular is because the announcer's voice is brimming with so much enthusiasm that the buyer thinks, "Well, maybe this is something to be excited about."

If the announcer's excitement about these $9.95 items can rub off on the viewer, thus prompting a sale, how excited should an agent be while selling a piece of real estate valued at $100,000 or more?

I don't suggest that you act like a carnival barker when you're with a buyer. But don't be afraid to show excitement about your product. After all, as Gerald O'Hara told his daughter, Scarlett, in *Gone With the Wind,* "Land is the only thing worth living for, worth fighting for, worth dying for, because land is the only thing that lasts."

That's more than can be said about a pocket-sized fishing rod.

Agents don't have to fight and die for sales and listings. But they shouldn't be opposed to showing enthusiasm. They might find that it's contagious, and that certainly can't hurt.

What agents accomplish as salespeople often depends not on what they say, but how they say it. That's called showmanship. It's easy to possess and even easier to develop with these simple pointers:

1. *Use prospects' names often.* Notice I said names. Don't direct all comments to Mr. Woochkowski if Mrs. Woochkowski is also present. And if she isn't, the agent shouldn't be there, either. The appointment should be scheduled so the agent can catch both prospects at home. But signatures will be needed, so agents might as well talk to both prospects at the same time.

2. *Use visuals.* Agents should never tell prospects anything that they can show them, instead. There is no way in the world an agent can make a point verbally as well as he or she can with words and pictures or other visuals. Why do you think television destroyed radio in the field of comedies, dramas and mysteries? And look at the fledgling, but ever-strengthening, video music industry. Using visuals can greatly improve the odds of getting a listing or making a sale, because they will allow an agent to communicate better with a prospect. You've heard it said that "A picture is worth a thousand words." For our purposes, let's paraphrase that to say, "A picture is worth a thousand dollars."

3. *Ask a lot of questions.* Agents should show interest in their prospects, and, at the same time, learn helpful information they can later take to the bank. Asking questions keeps the agent in control. The answering prospects are kept in a high level of interest because they are talking about their own personal situations.

4. *Add face and voice to your words.* This actually is an extension of the concept of using visuals. Words alone don't say it all. It's like the girl on a date with her boyfriend, who becomes rather amorous while parked at Lover's Lane. She says, "John, please! Don't! Stop!" But a few minutes later, she might be saying, "John, please don't stop!" She's saying exactly the same words, but with an entirely different meaning. (And you can bet that her face and voice inflection changed between the two sentences!)

Agents should use their faces and voice inflections to convey emotion. If they're pleased or excited, they should let their faces show it. If they want to show concern, they should let their faces assist by simply opening their eyes and raising their eyebrows (both of them, not just one, unless they want their prospects to think they're up to something sneaky).

And for goodness sakes, don't be afraid to smile. Some agents tell me that smiling just isn't part of their personalities. But rest assured that in this business, a fake smile will get an agent a lot farther than a sincere frown.

THE RIGHT FLOOR-TIME ATTITUDE

Have you ever been told a real estate agent was "on the floor"? It sounds terrible.

Actually, being "on the floor" does not mean the agent has had one drink more than he or she could handle. It means the agent is in the office and is responsible for handling incoming calls. (In some parts of the country, "floor time" is called "up time" or "schedule time," but it means the same thing).

What a perfect way to get leads! Yet, I've seen agents get upset when the phone rings. They are writing a letter to their relatives, when, all of a sudden, the telephone rings, and they say, "Darn, there goes the phone!" They are right in the middle of something that will have absolutely no positive effect on this month's bills (unless they're hitting up a rich uncle for a loan), yet they curse because they're interrupted by an opportunity to earn money.

That's strange enough, in itself. But then, consider that studies show a person's attitude generally has a strong bearing on the outcome of a situation. So if an agent has a negative or resentful attitude when a prospect calls, chances are good the potential transaction will never materialize.

Develop the right floor-time attitude. If the telephone rings, think of it as a cash register—yours. Be cheerful. Thank the prospect for calling. After all, there might be some money in this for you.

14

If the caller is interested in selling a home and wants to talk with an agent, announce that you're the one for the job and make a listing appointment. It will be one of the easiest leads you'll ever have.

More than likely, it will be someone calling for information on an advertised house. This could be an opportunity for a commission. On the other hand, it could just be an idle looker who, if given the opportunity, will waste your time. If that's the case, the best advice I can offer comes paraphrased from the Bible, which can be used as an effective sales manual—seek not the living among the dead.

Remember: A real estate agent's time is money. It shouldn't be wasted. So for heaven's sake, don't automatically set a time to meet the prospective buyer at the house. At this point, you don't know whether the caller is "living" or "dead." If the caller is just looking, a few probing "wopen" questions will get the caller off the line immediately. If you lose the prospect then, you've lost nothing except an opportunity to waste your time. In that case, you're better off cranking out that letter to your rich uncle.

Perhaps the caller is serious and plans to buy a house. And statistics show that someone who calls a real estate office about an advertised home actually will buy one within ninety days. But national studies also show that ninety-five percent of the time, the purchased home isn't the one in which the caller first expressed an interest.

So what do you do? Get the prospective buyer into your office. It's amazing that so many real estate agents don't know this, but it's the best way to:

1. Separate lookers from buyers.

2. Qualify the serious buyers.

Should a caller flatly refuse to come to the office, then you've got a decision to make. Do you gamble your time by showing a house the caller asked about, knowing that there's a ninety-five percent chance the caller won't buy (or can't afford) it? Or do you get back to that letter to your rich uncle? Only you know the odds on that.

CONVERT BUYERS INTO SELLERS

A principle that can generate a whole string of business is very simple, yet many real estate agents never think about it: Learn how to convert buyers into sellers.

Of course, this won't work on first-time home buyers. They have nothing to sell. But for those who already have a home, yet want to buy another, their best interests might be served by convincing them to sell immediately.

Many buyers wait for "that right house" to come along before they put their homes on the market. But this is a mistake. And you can score some points by showing them why. Many prospective buyers are reluctant to put their homes on the market because:

1. They don't want to rush.

2. They are afraid the house will sell too quickly.

3. They want to save money.

Show them some logic. First, why not rush? Of course, there is no fire, but if they want to make a move, why not now? Land isn't getting any cheaper, and only God and Chase Manhattan Bank know where interest rates will go tomorrow.

Second, in some areas, a house listed at full market value is likely to take six months or more to sell, according to national studies. That's plenty of time to look for that special house. What if the house does sell quickly? The buyer gets top dollar. Nothing wrong with that, is there?

Finally, they want to save money. Suppose the prospective buyer waits until finding "the right house" before placing the present residence on the market. Let's say "that right house" is found tomorrow, but it's listed at $5,000 more than the buyer wants to pay for it. What chance does the buyer have of persuading the new house owner to knock off $5,000, plus agree to hold the property for several months until the current residence can be sold? Slim to none.

Not only will waiting lessen the buyer's negotiating leverage, but it also will cost the buyer some cash on the current residence. To price a home for fast sale, several thousand dollars might have to be subtracted from the full market value to attract buyers instantly.

The bottom line? The prospective buyer has lost at least $7,000 by waiting. Yet, in the buyer's mind, the reason for waiting is to save money.

The public has so many misconceptions about what is wise and prudent when it comes to real estate. The more you can explode these myths and misconceptions, the better agent you will be and the more frequent your sales.

THE POWER OF PERSISTENCE

Once upon a time, door-to-door salesmen would stick their feet into doorways to prevent residents from slamming doors in their faces. But they eventually learned that, although effective, the technique was extremely hard on their feet. So they started thrusting their heads into the doorways. That way, if the prospect closed the door on them, they could keep right on talking.

Fortunately, the real estate business is a little more sophisticated than the old days of door-to-door salesmen. But some of the same principles still apply. The persistent salespeople will be the ones who walk off with the rewards.

The following statistics are true from coast to coast. Roughly eighty percent of the real estate agents will share twenty percent of all commissions this year. The other twenty percent will share eighty percent.

What does one agent in five have that sets him or her so far ahead of the other four? Persistence!

Wouldn't it be wonderful if every lead automatically and without great effort resulted in a listing or a sale? Of course, it would. But as a rule, that just doesn't happen. Remember how much selling an agent has to do just to get a sale? There are prospects who, for whatever reason, will not make decisions right away. They say they want time to think, or they ask you to call back three to six months later.

Suppose it's autumn, and a prospect tells you to call in the spring. So like a good agent, you wait. And when you call back, the conversation goes something like this:

"Hello, Mr. Prospect? . . . This is Joe Brown with On Track Realty . . . Joe Brown . . . That's right, B-R-O-W-N. You remember, I called you last Fall. . . . Yeah, I knew you'd remember. You said then for me to call you in the spring, because you thought you might be ready to move. . . . Oh, you have already? . . . And you got to keep the same telephone number, too? . . . But I thought you said you weren't going to move until the spring. . . . Oh, you met another agent, eh? . . . And the agent talked you into buying right away? . . . Waiting costs money, he told you? . . . I certainly agree with that. Well, I guess you won't need to hear from me again, then, will you? . . . No, I didn't think so. Well, it's been very nice talking with you, Mr. Prospect, and if you ever do need a real estate agent again, just give me a call.''

Waiting certainly does cost money. In this case, it cost our unfortunate friend, the agent, a commission.

Understand that the key to working with prospects is to follow up. If you can't immediately find the house to suit the prospect, don't give up. Keep looking and stay in touch. Don't give another agent the chance to sell the prospect a house before you do.

Call your buying prospects every month to keep abreast of their situations and to let them know what's available. If the prospects are potential sellers, call once a month to let them know you're still interested in handling the listings.

If you think this is pressure, you may be pleased to know that you are in a majority. It is indeed pressure, according to seventy percent of all new real estate agents. But we know what happens to them. They don't stay real estate agents for long.

Persistence works. If you plan to stop at the first "no," you may as well not even call. The amount of money to be made in real estate is in direct proportion with the salesperson's willingness to persist beyond the first rejection.

THERE'S A TIME FOR DREAMING

You don't want to be among the seventy percent of real estate agents who wash out. In fact, you want to be among the top producers. And you can, if you work at it. But don't forget to dream a little, too.

Remember when you were a child, and your parents would tell you to clean your room. It was something that had to be done, but it might have taken you all day to do it. You'd find all kinds of reasons to procrastinate.

But suppose your parents said, "When you finish cleaning your room, we're going to take you uptown for ice cream, then we'll go to the park." How long did it take to get your room clean then? Maybe an hour at the most. Why? Because you had a clear reward in mind while you were working.

That's why you should take the time to dream a little. For five minutes each day, relax, close your eyes and think about the things you want out of life. This will help establish a clear reward in your mind, which will serve as incentive to work hard—and smart.

How much money do you want to earn this year? Write it down and tuck it away somewhere, just for a reminder. Remember, the amount of money you earn depends on what you do, and what you do depends upon your activity.

The mind is an incredibly powerful motivator. If it can conceive, you can achieve. Yet, scientists say that people use only a fraction of their mental potential. A noted psychologist claims the average human being has more than enough brain power to learn forty languages, memorize a complete set of encyclopedias and complete the required course work for dozens of colleges.

You can actually strengthen your mind by challenging it. And if you take the principles in this book and study them again and again, they can become second nature to you, all by the power of repetitive learning.

But don't forget to dream a little. You need the promise of reward to keep you motivated.

BE YOURSELF

The story goes that back in the early 1940s a group of actors and studio personnel were shooting the breeze when one of the actors, a young man by the name of John Forsythe (who has become a household name through ABC's "Dynasty") started doing imitations of Humphrey Bogart, who by that time had achieved superstar status.

One of the members of the crowd thought he would have a little fun at Forsythe's expense. This man knew Bogie, and he knew the actor was on the lot filming a motion picture. So he left and returned minutes later with Bogie for the express purpose of watching Forsythe mimic the "tough-guy" star.

Talk about pressure! Here was Forsythe, a virtually unknown actor, who was about to mimic one of the greatest movie stars of all time—in his presence. He probably would have liked to have vanished from the face of the earth. Not being able to do that gracefully, he started his impressions. And he continued while everyone in the room, including Bogie, watched.

When he was finished, there was dead silence. All eyes in the room, especially Forsythe's, were on Bogie, whose stone-faced expression had not eased throughout the young actor's impressions. Finally, Bogie offered comment in that trademark raspy lisp that earned him $200,000 per picture (which at the time was a fortune, indeed).

"One of us shtinks," he said, leaving the room.

It's true, there was only one Humphrey Bogart. There's also only one Floyd Wickman. But never forget, there is only one "you," too.

This is not psychological pabulum to bolster your ego. Your self-esteem will soar when you realize that no one can do anything exactly like you can. And when you develop your own unique style, you'll do what you can in a way that no one else ever will be able to duplicate.

By the same token, if you try to imitate anyone else, you'll fall flat on your face.

Be yourself! You'll be more relaxed and, most importantly, so will your prospects. Try to imitate Bogart and your prospects may think you have problems and dismiss you on that basis.

COMMITMENT COUNTS

The best philosophy you should adopt is commitment. Dedicate your energies to real estate sales. Most people fail in this business because it's too easy to get in, and it's too easy to get out. They think, "Well, if this doesn't work, I can go back to my old job."

If that's your attitude, you will go back. You can count on it.

Success doesn't come easily. Often, it's a process of taking three steps forward and two backward, three more steps forward and two backward. It may take a while, but eventually, you'll get there.

Such is the path of a winner. On the other hand, there is the path of the loser, who takes two steps forward, then three backward, two more steps forward, then three more backward. You get the picture. In the final analysis, the loser will finish way behind the starting point.

The quickest route to success is running away from failure. Make the commitment to stay in the business. If you allow yourself the option to fail, you will. Failing is easier than succeeding.

In this chapter, I've tried to give you some basic philosophies to follow. The "meat and potatoes" of listing and selling real estate follow in upcoming chapters. If you're having trouble making that commitment now, read on. You'll see why it doesn't take special talents to sell real estate, and why you have every reason in the world to believe—just like the little steam engine—that you can climb that hill, too.

Then you can trash that letter to your rich uncle, because you're going to end up with more money than he has.

IN A CAPSULE

Here are a baker's dozen of pointers derived from the previous chapter that will help you lay the foundation for a successful career in real estate. Take these principles to heart, and you'll stay in the business long after others have failed.

1. Develop a positive mental attitude. There is no room for negative thinking in the real estate business.

2. Develop a logical mental attitude. You can't properly advise clients if you don't know the logic behind the real estate business.

3. Build an inventory of houses to sell. It's the first step to all real estate success stories.

4. Canvass by telephone. You'll reach more prospects faster.

5. Know how to sell. There is so much selling that goes into a sale.

6. Ask questions. It breaks the ice and gives you valuable information.

7. Learn showmanship. If you aren't excited about your product, no one else will be, either.

8. Develop the right "floor-time" attitude. Don't let a bad mood cost you a commission.

9. Convert buyers into sellers. Know how to influence prospects to act now.

10. Be persistent. If you're not, you're likely to be forgotten.

11. Dream. Set goals. They will inspire and motivate you.

12. Be yourself. You can't be anyone else nearly as well as you can be yourself.

13. Make a commitment. Don't plan to fail; vow to succeed! It makes a difference.

List the most important points you have gained from the preceding Strategy:

_____

_____

_____

_____

_____

_____

_____

_____

_____

_____

_____

_____

_____

_____

_____

_____

_____

_____

2

Work Smart, Save Time

Do you have enough time for work and your family, too? Are you working twelve-hour days, six and seven days each week, just to pay your bills? Are you finding yourself wishing there were more than twenty-four hours per day? Do you feel you don't have enough time to accomplish all you would like?

The story is told about the man who often played golf with his priest. One day, the man said, "Father, you have a closer connection with God than I do. Could you find out for me whether there are any golf courses in heaven?"

The next week, the priest looked up his friend and said, "Listen, I've got good news and bad news for you. The good news is, yes, there is a beautiful eighteen-hole golf course in heaven. The bad news is, you tee off tomorrow at eight-thirty in the morning."

Now here was a man who learned he really didn't have enough time to do what he wanted. Any of us could be in the same position. We could "tee off" tomorrow, too, but the odds are against it. So we're back at square one. We need more time, or at least we think we do.

The fact is: Nobody knows how many days you have left, but you're only going to get twenty-four hours for each. And you don't need more.

Just how busy are you? Are you so busy that you need more time than others? History speaks for itself. Benjamin Franklin discovered electricity. Thomas Alva Edison invented, among other things, the light bulb. Alexander Graham Bell invented the telephone. Jonas Salk developed a successful polio vaccine. Madame Curie discovered radium. Wilbur and Orville Wright made the first successful flight with a motor-powered machine, the forerunner of the airplane. Christopher Columbus discovered America (although he didn't know it at the time).

Every one of these people had only twenty-four hours per day to do what they needed to get done. And they did it! So just how much time do you need to make a living selling real estate? Rather than wishing there were more hours in a day, you'll fare better by using time to your best advantage.

If you think you aren't doing that, don't feel like the Lone Ranger. At a large sales rally several years ago, seventy percent of the five thousand people present indicated they would like future conventions to include time management seminars.

You are not alone. Many salespeople I meet seem to think they are disorganized. And if they *think* they are disorganized, they probably are too much so. It's not that they aren't working. They're working hard. They put in all the hours and attend all the meetings. But they are not working smart.

LET TIME SERVE YOU

There's a true story about a prison inmate. He was serving a fifteen-year sentence, so he decided to start his own tailoring business.

And he had, pardon the pun, a captive clientele consisting of other inmates who grew tired of general-issue uniforms. From there, he started serving guards, the clerical staff and, eventually, even the warden himself.

The man literally attained a fortune. After all, he was getting free room, board and medical care. And he didn't have to worry about putting gas in his car or spending money on entertainment. When asked what motivated him to amass such wealth, the inmate replied, "I decided that, instead of serving time, time would serve me."

You've often heard that time is money. But which is more valuable to you? If you've made money through ingenuity and persistence, then blow it, you can always make more money because you'll still have the know-how. But a day wasted is a day gone forever. God gives each of us twenty-four hours per day. We can spend them wisely, or we can waste them.

One way many people waste time is by worrying about a blunder they made yesterday, as if they can change the past if they worry long and hard enough about it. Or they may worry about what's going to happen tomorrow, never pausing to realize that all the worrying in the world won't enable them to gaze into the future and find out.

You can't do either of those things. So why try? It's wasted effort. And in so doing, you cheat yourself out of today—the only time that you'll ever have, the only time that your efforts actually can make any difference at all.

If it's a good month you want, you're only going to get it by doing your best every day for four weeks in a row.

ACCOUNT FOR YOUR TIME

Only you can control how you spend your time. And if you feel that you haven't been doing a good job at that, here's an exercise that may help: Get a sheet of paper and write down everything you did during the past three days that had absolutely nothing to do with making money. This includes everything from watching television, taking a nap, mowing the yard, going to the grocery, daydreaming, stopping by a bar and so on.

Circle all the things on that list that really weren't necessary. For example, mowing the lawn doesn't make you any money, but doing it on a regular basis keeps rats off your property and the neighbors off your back. Total the time that those non-necessary activities consumed, and you'll get an idea of where your time goes.

Let me illustrate my point. Have you ever been bitten by an elephant? Of course not. Because, as my colleague, Joel Weldon, observes, elephants don't bite. But you've surely been bitten by a mosquito or a gnat. You must beware of the little things, because they have a tendency to bite.

Wasting time involves the same principle. It's the fifteen minutes you spent on the telephone chatting with a friend. It's the extra half-hour you took at lunch, and the hour you spent at the bar. Add all those up and you've got two hours that you didn't devote to making money.

Remember: Elephants don't bite. It's the little things that will get you. It's like the man who smokes four packs of cigarettes each day. He would never even consider jumping off a fifteen-story building. But thirty or forty years down the road, he may develop a strong case of lung cancer that will cancel out all his tomorrows. In the end, it's the little things that get you.

Do you know that just fifteen minutes per day wasted totals to eleven full eight-hour days per year? If you're behind, how much work could you get done if, all of a sudden you were given eleven free days to catch up? If you use your time wisely, you won't need them.

This doesn't mean you have to become the living embodiment of Ebenezer Scrooge. After all, occasional small talk is good for office morale, which contributes to good working conditions. But if you work for someone, you really should work. And in the real estate business, you're actually working for yourself. Sure, your broker gets a cut of the sale, but your income depends solely on your production. So if you waste time, you're actually cheating yourself.

You don't have to work twelve-hour days, six and seven days per week. How boring! All work and no play makes Jack a dull boy. When you develop productive habits, you can afford to take two days each week to yourself. And when you've truly worked the other five, you'll enjoy those two days off so much more.

FLOUNDER OR TROUT

Before we review some time-saving tips, let me first ask you an important question: Are you a "flounder person" or a "trout person"? Before you decide, let's take a look at the characteristics of each fish.

The flounder lies on the bottom of the sea, waiting for its food to come along. It allows the tides to control its movements, and it does not resist natural forces. Consequently, it can easily be caught.

The trout swims against the currents, chooses carefully what it will eat, decides when to resist and when to rest and, consequently, is very difficult to catch.

Correspondingly, the "flounder person" reacts only to what comes his or her way. The "trout person" acts with forethought and self-discipline. The "flounder person" waits for something to happen, while the "trout person" makes things happen. The "flounder person" concentrates on activities, and the "trout person" concentrates on goals and objectives.

So what kind of a person are you? If you're not a "trout person," you can be. To take charge of your life, you must learn to control your habits, don't let them control you.

To control your time habits, consider these practical tips. Commit to applying them in your professional career to make the best of your time.

1. *Keep a time log.* No matter what you do, record it, along with the amount of time spent doing it. Keep the log long enough, and you'll find yourself making the most of every day by avoiding unnecessary and unfulfilling activities. If you work best under supervision, this log can be your "supervisor." It will be a viable tool to help you answer to yourself.

2. *Avoid people who would have you waste time.* It seems that in every group, there are certain people who never feel like working. But they usually don't want to be idle alone. They want company. So they grab anyone within reach to join them at some nonproductive activity.

   These people don't pay your bills. (They may not even pay their own!) And remember that you are responsible for your own bills, unless you write nice letters to your rich uncle! One idea that worked for me is to take an index card and draw a big dollar sign ($) on it. Then kindly inform everyone in your office that when they see that sign displayed by your telephone, it means you're in the process of making money and would rather not be disturbed.

3. *Work smart.* Working hard is fine, as long as you're working smart, too. Consider the case of the man who hired a lumberjack who could cut down an acre of trees per day, using only an ax. The man gave the lumberjack a chain saw and put him to work. At the end of the day, the lumberjack had cut down only three trees. His boss immediately wanted to know why he was working so slowly. The lumberjack said the chain saw was no good. He wanted his ax back. So the boss pulled the

cord on the chain saw and started it. The lumberjack's eyes opened really wide, and he asked, "What's that noise?"

You may work as hard as you'd like, but if you don't work smart, you'll merely spin your wheels. For optimum effectiveness, you should work in a manner that will produce the best results in the shortest period of time.

4. *Finish what you start.* Take a sheet of paper and draw a series of half-circles. When you're finished, you should have several "C's" on your paper. Those "C's" represent a visual presentation of a disorganized person's lifestyle.

All too often, people initiate projects they never finish. Aside from being unproductive, they are starting a habit that can drive them crazy. Psychiatrists say the leading cause of nervous breakdowns is leaving tasks and projects unfinished. Such people are so burdened with these unfinished tasks, they simply don't know where to start. So they keep procrastinating until, one day, nothing seems to matter anymore. All those unfinished projects just lower their already low self-esteem. Every task left undone is a reminder that they blew it once again.

Winners are good at what they do because they start productive projects, and they see them to the end. In the process, they save time and enjoy the rewards of success.

5. *List your priorities daily.* Then, rank each of them in order of importance. For example, if there are five tasks at hand, list them in the order you need to do them. Tackle number one first. Don't proceed to number two until you've finished number one. Don't touch number three until number two is finished, and so on.

Repeat this every day, and you'll be spending your days doing only what is most important . . . not merely responding to that which is urgent.

6. ***Invest your time with your best prospects.*** Determine the most likely prospect from whom you'll get a commission and deal with that one first. But how do you determine that? Rank them carefully by assessing their financial abilities and motivations to relocate. Let's say you have four prospects: the Browns, the Smiths, the Greens and the Whites.

The Browns are a new couple in town, having been transferred recently from another city. They've already sold their home and are currently living in a motel. This is a couple with a strong motivation and the financial resources to buy. Give them a plus in both categories. That makes them your top priority. In a matter of days, they're going to buy a house, and they're going to buy it from whoever shows them the one they like first. It might as well be you.

The Smiths, on the other hand, are currently residing in a high-crime area. They want to move to a better neighborhood. They rate a plus under the motivational column. Unfortunately, they have very little equity in their current home. Their combined incomes don't add up to a great deal of money. So they get a minus in the financial category. Rank them as number two. But circumstances can change. They could become a number one priority tomorrow. One of them could land a better job, or a rich uncle could die and bequeath them a fortune. They're worth one telephone call each week to keep track of their situation. If and when their financial ability changes, the Smiths will have two pluses to their credit, making them a top priority with any real estate agent who wants the commission.

The Greens get a big plus in the financial column. They have $75,000 in the bank, and their home is practically paid off. But they have a specific need—a century-old farmhouse, completely remodeled on twenty acres of land within five minutes from the city. If they can't find it, they will remain quite happy in their present home. Give them a minus under motivation. But keep your eyes on the fringes of the city, so you can be the agent who turns that number three priority into a commission.

And finally, the Whites. They're happy in their present home, but they'd like something a little nicer. They usually don't have anything to do on Sundays, so they don't mind looking at new houses. But they don't have very much equity in their present home, and the houses they tour generally are out of their price range.

Give them a minus in both categories. But don't write them off. Next month, the state may announce plans to cut a highway right through their front door. Suddenly, both minuses would become pluses overnight.

With this basic plan, you can learn to qualify your buyers. Then you'll get in the habit of investing most of your time and effort with the highly motivated, financially able prospects. As a result, you will sell a higher percentage of the homes you show.

Always keep in touch with your prospects. If and when they are able to make a purchase, what agent are they likely to call? That's right, the one who already has taken the preliminary steps with them. So never throw away your prospect cards. Keep them in your files.

7. *Keep an orderly filing system.* There are basically three kinds of filing systems, two of which are really more trouble than they're worth:

a. *The unorganized file:* "Hot prospects" are placed by the telephone, to be called right away. Investment buyers go into the top right-hand drawer, and cash buyers are in the pile with the corners torn off. It takes time to shuffle through all those cards. That's time you could be using on the telephone with a more organized system.

b. *The organized file:* It is, indeed, more organized; perhaps too much so. It consists of three of the most beautiful file boxes you've ever seen, and they all seem to make sense. File box number one contains an alphabetical listing of prospects. Should the prospect call the agent, the card can readily be located. But prospects rarely call agents, unless it's on a first-time basis. So, for the most part, this file is a waste of time.

File box number two sorts prospects in terms of financial abilities. Categories range from 0 to $29,999, $30,000 to $34,999, $35,000 to $38,999, $39,000 to $42,999 and so on, all the way to $999,999. The purpose is to help an agent find a qualified prospect after touring a particular house on the market.

Then there's the third file box with categories including two-bedroom homes, three-bedroom homes, three bedrooms and basement, two bedrooms and garage, two to three bedrooms and so on. But there are problems with this filing system, too. Remember, studies show that ninety-five percent of your prospects don't know what they want until you show it to them. They may tell you they need three bedrooms and a basement, only to end up buying a two-bedroom home with a garage. They may tell you they will spend no more than $70,000 on a home, then they'll find one they like at $85,000 and buy it right away. In short, people are going to buy the first home they see that they like and can afford.

c. *The prospect categorized by number file:* This is the best filing system I know. It takes no time to maintain, and it keeps you in touch with your prospects on a regular basis. Place each prospect card under the number that corresponds with the date. Then call each prospect once each month. (Sure, you'll have to double up at the end of months with thirty or fewer days, but you can handle it.) This file system is all you need.

Let's say today is the tenth day of the month. You call a prospect, and you're told to call back in three months. Put the prospect's name under number ten in your filing cabinet and call the prospect back on the tenth of next month. If you don't stay in touch with your prospects at least once a month, you risk losing them. Even if they tell you to call back next season, call them once a month. If you wait and call them when they ask, you may get an "I'm sorry, but the number you have reached is no longer in service. . . ."

Prospects rarely call agents. Even if they tell you to call them in three months or so, that doesn't mean they won't make a move without you. You can bet your commission on that.

8. *Learn how to close.* We'll save the "meat and potatoes" on this one for the last chapter of the book. But let's look at the benefits right now to emphasize the importance of time-saving.

Suppose you're on a listing appointment, and the seller stalls with the old "I-want-to-think-about-it" routine. So you go back next week, and the seller stalls again. At the end of the week, you go back and get the listing. Should you be elated? No. Oh, you can be happy that you got the listing, but look how much time it took you to get it. The time spent with the second and third visits could have been used for visits to other prospective sellers. And, if you were adept at closing, you could have had three listings for the time and effort you spent getting that one. True, you worked hard for it. But it will earn you no more money than it would if you had landed it the first time.

I don't want to sound like a broken record, but it's not necessarily the hard workers who get ahead. The smart workers who make the best use of their time are the ones who succeed. Treat time like you would money. Don't waste it, and there will be plenty to take care of your needs.

IN A CAPSULE

The following are eight tips derived from this chapter. Follow these suggestions to ensure that you'll make the most money in the least amount of time possible.

1. Keep a time log. You'll develop discipline in selecting your activities.

2. Avoid people who would waste your time. They don't pay your bills.

3. Work smart. Hard work alone won't take you where you want to go.

4. Finish what you start. You'll not only make more money, but you'll have peace of mind.

5. List your priorities every day. Then you'll only do what is important.

6. Spend your time with your best prospects. That's where the money is.

7. Keep an orderly filing system. Let it serve you; don't spend your time maintaining it.

8. Learn how to close. The better you are at it, the more money you'll make in less time.

For a quick reminder, it would be a good idea to list these eight tips on a note card, to which you can refer at any time. If you take to heart these principles, you'll find yourself working smart every day, which is what it takes to succeed in this business.

List the most important points you have gained from the
preceding Strategy:

_____

_____

_____

_____

_____

_____

_____

_____

_____

_____

_____

_____

_____

_____

_____

_____

_____

3

Build a Strong Inventory

Where is the worst place in the world to look for a real estate prospect? The graveyard! (Remember the Bible's warning about the living among the dead?)

Beyond that, there is no bad place to find prospects. Sure, some places are better than others, but even the worst place is good, as long as you can find prospects there.

When looking for prospects, you've got to take the attitude of young Michael Reilly from the New England area. He went to confession one day and said, "Father, forgive me, I have committed hanky-panky."

Of course, the priest wanted to grant Michael absolution, but first he asked the name of the woman.

"Was it Mary at the bakery?" the priest asked.

"No, Father."

"Was it Susie at the library?" the priest persisted.

"No, Father, not her," Michael responded. "I'm sorry, Father, I just can't bear to tell you."

"Very well, my son," the priest said. "But I'll want to see you next week."

Michael was leaving the church when he ran into a friend who knew why Michael had gone there.

"Hey, Michael, did you get absolved?" the friend asked.

"No," Michael said. "But I got a week off and two good leads."

I'm not suggesting that you do anything wrong to get a lead. But there's really no wrong way to get one. And this is good, because to become a top-notch real estate agent, you first must become a top-notch prospector.

It's amazing how many new real estate agents can't, or won't, accept this point. They want the listings, they want the money, and they want to do all the right things to get them—except for the very first step of lining up prospects.

This makes about as much sense as yearning to be a surgeon but not wanting to cut. Sounds silly, doesn't it? Yet, seventy percent of all new real estate agents have trouble with this initial step.

You have to crawl before you walk, and nothing worthwhile is ever easy at first (if it ever is at all). But some methods definitely are easier—and more productive—than others, and these will be the ones with which we'll concern ourselves.

My experience as a real estate agent and as a trainer clearly taught me that there are four basic methods for cultivating prospects. They are telephone canvassing, expired listings, for sale by owners and listing farms. Let's look at each one in detail.

I. TELEPHONE CANVASSING

Probably one of the most basic sources of prospects can be reached by the telephone. This was mentioned in chapters one and two, but it's being mentioned again here to stress its importance. The telephone will allow you to reach more prospects faster than by any other means of canvassing.

Of course, most of your calls may not achieve productive results. Suppose you call someone who has no plans to buy or sell in the near future. Have you wasted a call? Not really.

Circumstances can change. How many times in your life have you thought you were settled into a permanent situation, only to find out in a relatively short period of time that it wasn't so "permanent" after all? The situation could have been a job, a friendship, a relationship, a marriage—or even a place of residence.

The point is, any good public relations you can generate for yourself can't hurt. And possibly, you may get a commission later because you took a few minutes to talk with someone who, at least at the time, was in no position to contribute to your financial advancement.

Just be pleasant while explaining the reason you called. Since the prospect knows you won't be trying to sell anything, he or she may relax and even open up to you. If that happens, spend a few minutes talking.

Nice guys don't finish last, if they're smart.

Of course, not everyone you call will be nice. Some will be abrupt, others will hang up on you when they learn why you called and a few might even imply that your parents were never married. Forget them, at least for a while. You can always call them back later. The worst thing that can happen is they'll hang up on you again.

And consider how many people you can reach on the telephone. With a cross-reference or city directory, you can call number after number with no delay between calls. If you spend an average of three minutes per prospect (that's generous), you can reach twenty people an hour. No door-to-door prospector is going to cover that much ground in so little time.

And look at the psychological side of it. Suppose you and your spouse are at home, talking seriously about trading in the old car for a newer model. Suddenly, the phone rings. It's a local automobile dealership's salesperson who wants to know if you're at all interested in buying a car.

What are you going to think? "Hey, this is fate! I was just sitting here thinking about buying, and you call. Sure, I'm interested, when can we get together?"

It will be the same way when you reach a prospect who is ready to buy or sell. Of course, you may not find that prospect right away. You may have to dial a lot of numbers and get a lot of rejections first. But for a chance at $1,000 or so, how many numbers are you willing to dial? As many as it takes, I hope, because that's what it takes to get started in this business.

II. EXPIRED LISTINGS

Located within your multi-listings book is an expired listings section. This does not consist of people who died before their listed homes were sold. Instead, it's a collection of homes that recently were put on the market, but the listing expired before the houses could be sold.

Let's establish a point. An expired listing can be blamed on a maximum of two reasons—price and/or terms. One or both may have been unreasonable.

Occasionally, agents will say the reason a particular home doesn't sell is because of its location. Fine. They should pick up the house and move it to a place where it will sell.

It's not that simple, is it? If the location is bad, the price and/or terms must reflect it. No one will pay more than a house is worth. That's the main reason listings expire. And that's the best reason for you to avoid unsalable listings.

But not every agent can avoid them all of the time; hence, the expired listings. You can use them to find new prospects. It's not likely that the owner of a home with an expired listing will re-list with the same agent. No matter how ridiculous the price and/or terms, the original agent is going to be the villain in the eyes of the homeowner, because the agent couldn't sell the home.

This doesn't mean the seller won't cut the price or ease his terms. Perhaps some gentle persuasion is needed, and you can be the agent who can do it. And the original agent's time is on your side. The seller may have waited anywhere from three to six months for a sale that never materialized. By now, the seller may be a bit more reasonable (especially if he or she is growing impatient and is anticipating a move).

III. FOR SALE BY OWNERS

Check your local newspapers for prospects. Look under the classified advertising section of house sales or, if applicable, "for sale by owners."

These are homeowners who want to sell their homes without help from real estate agents. Yet, they're a great source of potential business. National studies show that seventy percent of them eventually list with agents because they're either unwilling or unable to sell the houses themselves.

This means that seven out of ten would-be home sellers will be looking for an agent in the not-too-distant future. If you're lucky, maybe they'll select you from among all the agents in your area.

But why rely on luck? Improve your odds of being selected by calling them first. Sure, some of the ads might specifically say, "No agents." Don't let that discourage you. Those are the ones you should call. If nothing else, you can say, "Hey, I saw your ad that said "No agents," and that's why I'm calling. My broker says

I'm the closest thing to 'no agent' he ever saw.'' Or more realistically, ask the prospect if you could visit and offer some tips on selling the house.

The prospect immediately will ask why you would spend time helping to sell a house for which you will not receive a commission. And you can answer honestly by saying that, in exchange for your tips, you would like for the prospect to call you should he or she eventually list the house with an agent. This is called a "fair trade" offer. If the prospect accepts, you have a seventy percent chance of eventually getting a listing.

"For sale by owners" are a good and easy source of prospects. If there are thirty listed in your newspaper on a given day, odds are that twenty-one of them eventually will list with an agent. Those are great odds for agents who feel like calling. And the ads represent a good deal of possible commissions. You won't land all of them. But you'll get none of them if you don't try. And I hope you will at least try, because if you don't, twenty-one of your competitors may be getting the commissions that you willingly passed up.

IV. THE LISTING FARM

Almost everyone who enters the real estate business starts a "listing farm." This is a method of developing prospects that, if given proper attention, will continue to bring benefits over the years, so you won't have to work as hard in the future.

First, what is a "listing farm"? It's an area—a subdivision, half of a subdivision, neighborhood, etc.—that an agent "adopts" as a "personal" prospecting ground. The agent's job is to make contact with all the homeowners located within the selected area. So the "farm" should include enough homes to keep the agent busy, but not overworked. If properly developed, it's a great method of building an inventory.

All houses standing today have something in common. Eventually, they're going to be sold. Figures indicate that, in some areas, the average family relocated every three to five years. It's possible that ten to twenty percent of the homes in your "farm" may be put on the market within a year.

Your objective is to get everyone in the "farm" area to know your name and like you enough so that, if and when they decide to sell their houses, you will be the agent they call.

Sounds simple, doesn't it? So why do so many agents start a farm, then abandon it within a relatively short period of time? Mainly because they bite off more than they can chew. They decide that their "farm" is going to consist of the entire southeastern section of the city, or some area equally as vast. And then, because of the sheer size of the area and the number of homeowners that must be contacted, they get bogged down with confusion, and complications set in. Rather than deal with them, they just give up.

A large "farm" worked inconsistently is not as good as a small one that can be worked with a degree of regularity. Bear in mind that cultivating a listing "farm" does not take the place of any other form of prospecting. It is only a supplement. If you want to improve your odds at staying in the business, it must be done in addition to telephone prospecting and checking out expired listings and "for sale by owners."

The benefit of having a "farm" is strictly for public relations at first, unless you contact someone who is interested in selling a house. And if that happens, so much the better.

Even if that doesn't happen, you're not wasting time. Most people have a family doctor, a family dentist, a family attorney and maybe even a family accountant. But they don't have a family real estate agent, and history has shown that one day, they will need one.

So why shouldn't it be you? You can increase your odds of becoming a family's agent just by touching base with them.

Don't expect immediate results, though. That's another reason agents quit working with their "farms." They get tired of waiting. They don't persevere. It's just like planting and growing a garden.

It takes effort and patience. No one can watch a crop grow overnight. That's why "farming" should be done in addition to other forms of prospecting, so an agent won't starve. After all, if you were starving, you wouldn't depend upon a new garden to take care of your immediate need. But the food it eventually will yield certainly might come in handy later.

The same principle is involved with a listing farm. But how does one practically develop a workable "farm"? First, an area consisting of approximately fifty homes must be selected. Declare that area as your "farm."

Your objective is to get every one of those homeowners to know your name—first and last—within six months. You'll want it to become a household word, because one day, one of those homeowners is going to come home and say, "Honey, I've been transferred. We've got to move." Another may come in and say, "Baby, I've finally gotten that promotion. Let's move into that neighborhood up town like we've always wanted." And still another might say, "Dear, I'm pregnant. And this time, the doctor says it's going to be twins. We're just going to need another bedroom, and our lot here is too small to add on to the house."

Nothing is permanent. Situations change every day, and fifty or so homes add up to a lot of opportunities. When moving situations arise, the people involved will need a real estate agent. They can find dozens in the yellow pages. But if they've already become familiar with you, odds are good they'll call you.

Probably the best way to put all this to work in a meaningful way that will pay rich dividends over time is to develop a six-month plan. Here's a suggested format to follow.

A. *First month*—Meet all of the homeowners face-to-face. Several days each week, take an hour to ring doorbells and shake hands. Give each homeowner one of your business cards and introduce yourself and your company. In fact, your introduction could go something like this:

"Hello, my name is _____

from _____Realty. How are you today? I'm specializing in this neighborhood, but the purpose of my visit today is first of all, to introduce myself and also to tell you about the newsletter we'll be producing shortly. I'd like to know if you have any information you would like us to include, such as want ads, favorite recipes, announcements of special services like babysitting . . . anything of that nature."

Take the information, thank the prospects for their time, smile (always smile), shake hands again and go on to the next house, where you'll do the same thing again. That's it. Nothing difficult at all about it, and it doesn't hurt (unless you get bitten by an unruly Doberman pinscher).

So what did you accomplish? Nothing that you can take to the bank. Yet. What you have done is taken the first step toward getting the residents of your "farm" to know your name and to like you.

What's the benefit of the newsletter? It's the best tool there is for working a "farm." The homeowners get timely information about community affairs, and you get exposure, because your name will be displayed prominently upon it.

The next step is to compile the information and print the newsletter and distribute copies to residents of your chosen "farm."

B. *Second month*—Either mail the newsletter or hand-deliver it, depending on what you prefer and/or whatever is legal in your area. That's all.

C. *Third month*—Call every homeowner in your "farm" and ask them if they enjoyed the newsletter. Be sure to tell them who you are and what company you represent. That's all.

D. *Fourth month*—Return to the neighborhood for more door-to-door visits. Reintroduce yourself, tell the residents you're planning another newsletter and ask them for new information. While you're there, you can just happen to leave printed information about your company and its services. Also, you can leave a list of area properties that have recently been sold. Ask them to tip you off if they know anyone thinking of moving in or out of the area. Assure them you'll give the prospects your personal attention. Then go to the next house and repeat the process.

E. *Fifth month*—Send out the newsletter again.

F. *Sixth month*—Call the homeowners and ask if they liked the newsletter. Tell them about your prospective buyers who are considering moving to the area. Ask if they know of anyone thinking of moving out.

To summarize, here's what you've done over a mere six months:

- Fifty residents saw your face and heard your name.

- They saw your name again on the newsletter.

- They heard your name and voice over the telephone.

- They saw your face and heard your name again.

- They saw your name again on the newsletter.

- They heard your name and voice again over the telephone.

By this time, you've practically become a household word.

START NOW—AND WORK AT IT

If you plan to build a real estate career, start preparing your future. There are many organizations which provide real estate agents with newsletters. Your broker possibly can recommend some. If not, you can design one yourself with nothing more than a sheet of paper and a typewriter. Duplicates can be made on your office copying machine or at a local quick-print center. It's easy. It's economical. It pays off.

If you don't plan to work the "farm" consistently for six months, don't start one. You'll only be wasting your time. But if you can make a commitment to yourself right now, you'll be amazed at how much business your area will generate within a relatively short period of time. You may also find that you can have a lot of fun working your "farm." And having fun can be great when you're making money at the same time.

I hope that I made it clear in this chapter: There is no bad way to find prospects. You must work at it from all directions. If you want to write letters to all your friends and neighbors, that's fine. You may also want to send cards to all the organizations and clubs to which you belong. You may even want to touch base with everyone with whom you've ever done business. It can't hurt. But remember, if you stick to only those people who you already know, you'll get nowhere fast in the real estate business.

If you work (and unless you have a rich uncle, you must), you may as well work smart.

IN A CAPSULE

1. When it comes to finding prospects, any way you can find them is at least good. Some ways are even better than others. But the best methods are those that yield the greatest number of prospects in the shortest amount of time.

2. Learn to canvass by telephone. It's the best tool to search for prospects.

3. Study the expired listings. They consist of homeowners who, in all possibility, still want to sell their homes but are looking for a different agent to handle the transaction.

4. Don't be afraid to call "for sale by owners." Although they may not know it, seventy percent of them will be looking for a real estate agent in the not-too-distant future. Get your name in the hat early.

5. Develop a listing farm, but don't bother unless you commit yourself to working it. Like a regular garden, it can feed you when times are lean, if proper care is taken.

List the most important points you have gained from the
preceding Strategy:

_____

_____

_____

_____

_____

_____

_____

_____

_____

_____

_____

_____

_____

_____

_____

_____

NOTES

Section 2

LISTINGS—THE NAME OF THE GAME

4

Persisting for the Listing Appointment

Staying on the track is important.

If a runner during a race strays from the track, he or she will be disqualified. If a professional race car driver steers off the track, chances are good that driver, car, or both are experiencing trouble. If a train jumps the track the consequences can be serious indeed.

Do you know that real estate agents have tracks, too? And if they jump them, they can get into trouble. The consequences may not be as severe as for a derailed train, but it could cost them a commission.

That's severe enough, isn't it?

How does a locomotive engineer arrive at a destination? By staying on the track. How does the race car driver and the runner finish the race? By staying on the track.

How do you get the listing appointment? By staying on the track.

A track is just a step-by-step plan that agents use to accomplish their objectives. There are tracks for every aspect of the real estate business, including getting listings, handling callers who inquire about advertisements, demonstrating properties and closing on buyers.

By now, you already know how to find prospects. But what do you say to them when you call them? You're probably not going to demand immediately that they list with you. That wouldn't be the most persuasive approach.

You need an approach that offers a step-by-step plan to accomplish your objective—getting the listing appointment. The approach I'm going to offer won't result in an appointment every time. But for the most part, an agent can cut through a potential seller's resistance by staying on a track designed to make the seller feel good about making the appointment.

When prospecting, you never know what the prospect will say next. Consequently, you don't always know what you'll say next. But if you follow the prospecting track, one step at a time, you'll always be in control.

A lot of real estate agents are like Elizabeth Taylor's next husband. They know what's expected of them, they're just not sure they can deliver.

That's what a track does for you. It shows you, one step at a time, how you can deliver your message to the potential seller who, at least at first, may not be receptive to you.

STEP 1:
APPROACH

What kind of approach do you use? That's up to you. There are no bad ones, so long as they're honest and in good taste.

You shouldn't tell a prospect you don't want to list the house, that you only want to look at it. That's not true. And don't gain entry by promising to recommend the house to your buyers. Why should you do that until you get the listing?

STEP 2:
FAIR TRADE OFFER

A fair trade offer might entice the prospect into making the appointment with you.

In the case of a "for sale by owner," perhaps you could offer suggestions on how to sell the house in exchange for the seller's consideration to contact you should the house eventually be listed. And the odds are seven out of ten that's exactly what will happen.

Sometimes, you may have trouble convincing the prospect you indeed have a fair-trade offer. Occasionally, when I conduct seminars, I'll ask if anyone will trade fifty cents for a dollar. Very few people will usually take me up on it. The rest either will be too skeptical for their own good, or they just truly don't understand the good offer.

So you'll have to detail your intentions to your prospects. In exchange for future consideration, offer the "for sale by owner" some tips on financing, advertising and/or demonstrating the house.

When talking with the owner of a house with an expired listing, offer to point out some reasons why the property didn't sell. With a market analysis, you can show, more than likely, that the price and/or terms were unreasonable.

No matter with whom you are talking, your approach must include a fair-trade offer. Remember, prospects always want to know what is in it for them.

STEP 3:
EXPECT REJECTION, BUT PERSIST!

Carve those words into stone. You'll need persistence for every phase of this business. Remember how much selling it takes to lead to the actual sale itself.

No matter what approach you use, how honest it is, how smooth you sound and how much of a fair trade offer you offer, the first time you ask for the appointment, prospects virtually always will decline.

Somewhere out there is a seller's training school. There just has to be! I've met with real estate people all over North America, from little towns like Edmond, Oklahoma to cities such as Chicago. These agents tell me that different types of prospects use different initial rejections. "For sale by owners" generally say, "Thank you, but no, I don't need an appointment. I have a friend in the real estate business who already is giving me pointers." "Expired listings" usually say, "Thank you for calling, but we have decided to hold off for a while and wait to see what happens to the market." And "cold canvass" prospects say, "Call me in the . . ." and they pick the next season.

The average real estate agent will stop trying with the first rejection. Next month, the agent will wonder why that "for sale by owner" or "expired listing" has listed with a competitor. Or the agent really will call back those evasive prospects three months later, just to hear them say how much they are enjoying their new homes and that they definitely won't need another real estate agent for the rest of their lives.

The agents lost the listings, and the sales, because they weren't persistent. They stopped with the first rejection, while their competitors did not.

PROVEN TRACK

The track I'm offering here is designed to keep you comfortably on the telephone with prospects who may already have said they're not interested in appointments.

The words are not so important; you can use your own. The key is to be comfortable with the track, and, by all means, to be yourself.

Step One—Introduce yourself.

Tell the prospect who you are and what company you represent.

Step Two—Make your fair trade offer.

Entice the prospect into letting you make the appointment.

Step Three—Don't ask if you can visit.

Give the prospect a choice of times that you might visit. Don't ask, "Could I come over tonight?" Instead, try "Could I come over at six tonight, or would seven be better?" This is known in the business as an "alternate of choice close." A prospect is least likely to refuse an agent if given a choice of times, rather than the choice to accept or refuse the appointment.

Step Four—Expect initial rejections, but persist.

Keep asking questions. There are no bad ones. Any questions will do. "How long have you been trying to sell your house?" "How many bedrooms do you have?" "What's your dog's name?" Anything will do, as long as you keep prospects talking and interested long enough so that in a couple of minutes, you can try your fair trade offer again.

And if you get another rejection, don't quit. Ask more questions.

THE MAGIC OF PERSISTING

If you practice, drill and rehearse this four-step plan long enough, you'll become comfortable with it. And many times you'll find that persistence pays off in big ways.

You can expect the first rejection automatically. Maybe even the second one, too. But often, you'll find there is magic in asking three times.

Most agents ask only once. They're among the eighty percent of agents who split twenty percent of commissions. Learn to ask twice, and you'll get more appointments than you ordinarily would. But if you get into the habit of persisting—if you make a commitment to ask three times for the appointment—you'll get plenty of appointments with good prospects.

If you persist (in addition to practicing, drilling and rehearsing), you'll become strong on the telephone. This doesn't mean offensive. It means competent, confident and natural. Those are the best qualities any salesperson can have.

DON'T BLOW IT

One good way to get more listing appointments is by not losing them. Many agents develop fantastic leads, only to lose the prospects over the telephone because they say too much or the wrong thing. They'll tell the prospect how much they think the house is worth, how long they think it will take to sell it or what kind of commission they will get. Should one or more of their answers offend the prospect, there's no appointment.

So here's a tip. It's foolproof. No matter what question the prospect asks about the potential transaction, this answer will fit: "Gee, I don't know. I haven't seen your house yet. Let's get together."

That's it. Simple, isn't it? Multi-million-dollar producers don't rattle on with opinions and lose the appointments. They use this answer. It keeps the seller interested, and it's a lot easier than trying to play SuperAgent over the telephone.

"What do you think the house is worth?" the prospect asks. "Gee, I don't know. I haven't seen the house yet. Let's get together."

"How much commission will you get?" the prospect asks. "Gee, I don't know. I haven't seen the house yet. Let's get together."

"How long do you think it will take to sell my house?" "Gee, I don't know. I haven't seen the house yet. Let's get together."

If you have an interested prospect, don't blow it. Don't scare the prospect away by showing off your knowledge, or lack of it.

Know when to quit selling.

HOW TO REACH "FOR SALE BY OWNERS"

There are only three reasons why people try to sell homes without the services of a real estate agent. Excuses can take a dozen different forms, but generally, they all boil down to three reasons:

1.   The homeowner wants to save money.

2.   The homeowner is afraid of agents.

3.   The homeowner wants to save time.

The first reason, and most common, is the impetus for most "for sale by owners." They may say they're trying to save a commission, but they're actually trying to get more money for themselves. As a rule, you may assume that most of them are motivated by this reason.

The second reason gives all agents a black eye. The homeowner might know someone who had a bad experience with a real estate salesperson, which serves as the motivation for the seller to act as his or her own agent. Even that reason is linked to money, because what bad experience can a person have with a real estate agent that doesn't concern money? (Unless the agent was a psychopathic killer.)

The third reason—saving time—generally doesn't hold water. Perhaps one time in twenty, a homeowner will talk to three or four brokers, get an average price, deduct the commission and sell the house for that price. But most of the time, the sale takes time. And time is money, even for prospects, so even this reason concerns money.

Money is a powerful motivator. Use it to your advantage. But handle it with kid gloves. When you're talking with a "for sale by owner," understand there is quite an ego involved. The seller wouldn't be trying to sell the house, otherwise. You won't benefit by saying it can't be done.

So after getting the appointment honestly, impress the sellers any way you can. Use your smooth style, your knowledge, your humor . . . whatever it takes to get them to like and respect you. Then, follow up. Stay in touch. This works much better than scare tactics. They generally don't change the minds of "for sale by owners." Time generally takes care of that.

So make time work for you. Think about the process. A homeowner decides to sell a house, puts an ad in the newspaper and posts a sign on the front lawn. Two weeks, three weeks, a month to six weeks goes by, and the house still hasn't sold. The homeowner must do something—either cancel the move or select a broker to handle the sale.

There's a seventy percent chance that the seller will opt for the latter. If he or she already has met and talked with you, you'll be the likely candidate.

GET COMFORTABLE WITH QUESTIONS

Learn to ask questions. Aside from keeping your prospects interested, the time it takes them to answer will give you time to think and plan your next move.

Also, learn to phrase your questions so they are answered with a "yes." (Not your "open" questions, of course.) Studies show that the more a person can answer "yes" to the little questions, the easier it will be to get the person to say "yes" to the big questions.

Let's illustrate these principles through a monologue of an agent's side of a telephone conversation with a prospect.

Hello, is this the owner of the property advertised in today's news? My name is _____
from _____ Realty. I'd like to stop by and take a look at your house, as well as leave you some information that might help you sell it without a broker.

No, I'm not trying to get the listing. But I'm sure you are wondering what's in it for me. You see, studies show that seven out of ten homeowners who try to sell their own homes eventually list with an agent. Of course, I understand that you may actually sell your house yourself. Even if you sell it, I believe that if I do something of benefit for you, maybe you'll call me if you ever need, or know anyone who might need, a real estate agent.

Does that sound like a fair enough trade? Good. Can I stop by about six tonight, or would seven be better? Oh, I see, you have a friend in the real estate business, and you're getting tips from him.

How long have you been trying to sell your home? That's not bad. How often do you advertise? . . . I see. And where are you moving if the house sells? . . . Oh, that's a nice area, isn't it? . . . Why are you thinking about selling without a broker? . . . I see.

Suppose I could give you some tips on advertising your property so you could sell it faster. Would you at least give me a little time to review these tips with you? I could stop by about six, unless seven would be better.

Oh, I see. . . . You really are not interested in having any agents visit. Okay, in what newspaper are you advertising? . . . Just the News? Okay, have you had any deposits on your home? Have you had many people look at your home? What about your home did they not like? . . . Oh, they seemed to like it?

Okay, tell me if this isn't a fair trade. Would it be possible to come over, look at your home and offer some information that would help you sell it? What if I promised you I wouldn't ask for a listing unless you gave me permission? Could I stop by at six tonight, or would seven be better?

When an agent promises not to ask for a listing without the owner's permission, yet still offers some tips on selling the house, it's pretty difficult for a homeowner to refuse. And when you go to visit this homeowner, be sure you ask his permission to ask for the listing. After all, you never said you wouldn't do that. The worst thing the homeowner can do is order you to leave (unless he puts the Doberman on you).

WHEN YOU GET THAT APPOINTMENT

Once you've landed the appointment, pre-condition the seller. It doesn't matter whether it's a "for sale by owner," "expired listing," or "cold canvass." Detail for them step-by-step exactly what you plan to do during your appointment.

Tell them that, with their permission, you will ask a series of questions to find out about their likes, dislikes, wants and needs in regard to the sale. Tell them that you, with their permission, plan to tour the house to get an idea of what price it would bring.

Let them know you'd like to speak with them about the advantages of doing business with you and your company. Afterward, again with their permission, you would like to discuss pricing and terms, along with ironing out other details.

Then—and not before—you'll ask for a "yes" or "no" as to whether they want to list with you. Don't give them the option to say "maybe," because ninety percent of them will. Make it a simple "yes" or "no." And if you've done your job right, the same ninety percent will say "yes." You'll learn more about this process in the next chapter.

ONE-STOP LISTINGS

One of the best ways to work smart in the real estate business is by getting listings with just one visit.

This very statement often shocks a lot of real estate agents, even those who are very successful in the business. A very successful agent who signed up for one of my seminars said the best thing he got out of it was the benefit of saving time and effort with one-stop listings.

Most agents are accustomed to two-stop listings. They visit the first time to establish rapport and get enough information to establish a market analysis. Then they go back to the office and prepare the analysis, then return and talk price, terms and details.

But another reason many agents favor the two-stop listings is because they're apprehensive. They think it takes real nerve to expect a listing with just one visit.

A one-stop listing will save time, which can be spent getting another listing. And it only stands to reason that an agent that practices one-stop listings will earn twice as much as a colleague with equal skills who makes a habit of stopping twice.

The first question that comes to the skeptics' minds probably is, "How are we going to do a market analysis in just one stop?" Simple. Get enough information when making the appointment to establish a fairly accurate market analysis.

There are four things an agent must find out from the homeowner after the appointment has been set:

1. Enough information to establish a comparative market analysis.

2. Whether the seller indeed wants to sell. Many agents make a habit of giving away free appraisals.

3. Whether both spouses are going to be home or not. You need both signatures. If they're both there, that will cut down on the two-stop listings.

4. How much money the owner thinks the house is worth.

That last item might be a little tricky. The first time that question is asked, seventy percent of the prospects won't answer. They say, "You're the agent, you tell me."

Don't argue with them. Ask a few more questions. Any kind of question. Then ask them the question a different way—"What are homes like yours selling for?" Half of those who wouldn't answer at first will tell you.

But not all of them. There will be some who will hold out for your estimate. Not to worry. Ask a few more questions. Then find out the monthly payment and the mortgage balance. They may profess not to know, so ask them to give you a rough idea.

Then ask how much in-pocket cash the seller wants to net from the sale. Suppose the seller says, "If I can't get $40,000 in-pocket, I'm not selling."

Take $40,000 and add it to the estimated mortgage balance.

Then add several thousand dollars and you'll get the general price range.

For example, suppose the seller told you that roughly $32,000 remains to be paid on the house. Add $40,000 estimated in-pocket cash to $32,000 on the payoff and you can figure that the house is in the $75,000 to $80,000 range.

So right after you've finished reading this page, I want you to put down this book and get a copy of your local newspaper. Find the section that offers "for sale by owners" and call the first advertisement listed.

Don't procrastinate, and don't read all the ads to pick out the best one. The more you read, the more you will procrastinate and eventually rationalize why you shouldn't call.

I challenge you now to pick up the phone and call. Offer your fair trade and ask for the appointment. Persist, and ask at least three times. Make sure you understand that the reason they're trying to sell the homes themselves is to save money, or make more money for themselves.

If you take me up on this challenge, not only will you be another step closer to earning a commission, but it may well be a giant step toward your career. You will have formulated the fortitude that it takes to make the most important call—your first.

After all, there is a lot of money in "for sale by owners." Seven out of ten eventually will list with an agent, probably one who stays on track and perseveres.

Which agent? Might as well be you!

IN A CAPSULE

1. Most successful real estate agents stay that way by staying on track, a step-by-step plan designed to obtain for an agent a listing appointment. Don't be concerned so much with the words of the track as you should be with the concepts behind the track.

2. Any approach you can use to reach a prospect is fine, as long as it's honest and in good taste. Don't gain entry to the prospect's home by lying about a potential benefit.

3. Be sure the approach has a built-in fair trade offer for the prospect. Prospects always want to know what's in it for them.

4. Don't ask a prospect whether you can visit. Ask the prospect what time you can visit. An alternate of choice close boosts the odds of your getting the appointment.

5. Expect rejections, and learn to persist. Prospects virtually always refuse to make an appointment at first. Many times, you can land the appointment if you keep trying.

6. Reach the "for sale by owners" by impressing them with your knowledge, humor, style . . . any way you can! If and when they decide to list, you'll likely be their agent.

7. Learn to ask questions. It keeps your prospects interested and it keeps you in control.

8. Once you get a lead, know when to stop selling. Don't talk yourself out of an appointment by giving potentially volatile opinions as to how much you think the prospect's house is worth, or how much commission you may get for selling it. Learn to answer inquisitive prospects by

saying, "Gee, I don't know. I haven't seen your house yet. Let's get together."

9.   When you get the appointment, pre-condition the prospect by telling him or her exactly what you plan to do during the appointment. This gives the prospect an idea of what to expect, and it lends an air of professionalism to your style. Then let the prospect know that you will be asking for a "yes" or "no" answer in regard to whether he or she will list with you.

10.   After getting the appointment, find out from the potential seller on the telephone some basic facts about the house, so you can compile a market analysis before going over. This will help you save time and increase your odds of having one-stop listings.

List the most important points you have gained from the
preceding Strategy:

_____

_____

_____

_____

_____

_____

_____

_____

_____

_____

_____

_____

_____

_____

_____

_____

_____

5

Make the Most of the Listing Appointment

Remember your first airplane trip? Strange, wasn't it? Maybe even frightening.

There was good reason to be scared. First, it was a new experience, one that literally put your head in the clouds and took your feet away with it. Also, consider that the plane was built by the lowest bidder.

The fact is: Air travel is the safest method of long-distance transportation. Federal regulations stipulate that ground crews must check the craft from nose to tail to make sure everything is working perfectly. Once that big bird gets into the air, it may be too late to take action should something go wrong.

It's the same way when you are on a listing appointment. There are all kinds of preparations you can make to increase your chances of getting the listing.

Here's what the average real estate salesperson does when getting a listing appointment. And if you want to be average (I don't think you do), study these next several paragraphs.

The phone rings. The agent gets the listing appointment. Jumping up with all the enthusiasm of Clark Kent about to change into Superman, the agent yells to all within earshot that he has landed a listing appointment, grabs his briefcase and runs out the door.

What was in his briefcase? That doesn't matter as much as what wasn't in it. There was no market analysis, no partially completed listing agreement, no material promoting himself or his company. There was nothing in the briefcase except a half-written letter to his rich uncle and a copy of this book that he hasn't even opened yet.

Does he get the listing? He might. But chances are, he won't. But you know what he will say when he gets back to the office, when his co-workers look at him with anticipation and ask, "Did you get it?"

"No," he replies. He is Clark Kent again. But there is still that Superman dream in his mind, because he quickly adds, "But I will."

KNOW THE ODDS

If you don't get the listing the first time, odds are good you'll never get it. I know this not only from my own painful experience, but also from the tens of thousands of real estate agents who have attended my seminars, read my books and listened to my cassette learning systems.

If you've ever been to Las Vegas or Atlantic City to gamble, chances are you may have lost. And you lost for one reason and one reason only. The odds were stacked against you.

An agent leaving for a listing appointment without making the necessary preparation is like the pilot who takes off without first checking the plane. If either one runs into trouble, the appointment or the flight could end before its scheduled time, and its objective might not be accomplished.

True, you may not need anything to get the listing. In some cases, the seller is ready to list with you before you even arrive at the house. But what if you need extra material that you don't have?

The pilot has absolutely no need for a parachute, until the plane develops trouble in flight. When the moving van runs a red light, the oncoming motorcycle rider had better be wearing a helmet; it's too late to go home and get it.

It's like having a spare tire in the trunk of your car. You don't plan to have a flat. But if you do, you're at least prepared.

KNOW THE ENEMY

What if you were going to war, and someone handed you the key to a vast arsenal? You opened the door to find every kind of weapon—fighter planes, tanks, bazookas, hand grenades, machine guns, mortars, bombs. . . . What would you take with you? A .22-caliber pistol?

Of course not. You would take everything you could carry that would offer you the best protection. So what if you don't need them? Odds are, on the battlefield, you will need them. You can't dodge the enemy all the time. It's better to carry those weapons and not need them, rather than to leave them behind and wish that you hadn't.

In the real estate business, the enemy is any objection or stall that a prospect can hand you to justify any unwillingness to list or buy. So before you leave on your listing appointment, take with you all the weapons you can possibly use to lower your potential seller's resistance to giving you the listing.

WHAT WEAPONS TO TAKE

1. *Take along a partially completed listing agreement.* Ask the seller some basic questions over the telephone and conduct a bit of local research. That will help you to complete much of the agreement before you leave the office.

2. *Prepare a market analysis.* Determine how much other comparable homes have sold for recently and how much similar homes are selling for now. Get the asking prices for comparable homes with expired listings. This will help you and the seller start talking about the price. You will have some information to lend credibility to your price recommendation. Sellers often tend to have an overinflated sense of what their houses are worth. Your job is to bring them down to earth—gently.

3. *Use visuals pertaining to the real estate business.* You'll make your point better when you rely on a combination of both the verbal and the visual media. It's like Willie Sutton, the legendary bank robber who robbed more banks than anyone in U.S. history. Periodically, he would be apprehended. Once, a federal agent asked him why he robbed banks. "That's where the money is," Willie replied. The agent then asked him why he used guns, because weapons compounded the felony. "I find they're good visual aids," he reportedly responded. "The words, 'Stick 'em up' just don't deliver the proper impact without a strong visual aid." Use any visual aid that will help prospects decide to act. Expired listings and market analysis

are great for lending credibility to your recommended price. Printed material promoting yourself and your company can help convince the prospect to do business with you. Even newspaper articles on a positive economy can help persuade a prospect to act now.

4. *Carry a tape measure.* It's a good tool for showmanship, and it's great for accuracy. Also, it's a means to involve the seller. It takes both agent and seller to stretch a tape measure across a room.

5. *Have a seller's expense sheet handy.* This is a printed form which shows sellers what their expenses are.

6. *Bring actual photographs of similar houses that already have sold.* Should the seller balk at the price you recommend, you'll be able to show that similar houses were priced in the same range.

You may be able to think of six to eight other items. If you think they'll help you get the listing, by all means, take them along. Even if they accomplish nothing else, these items will give you greater confidence on the listing appointment. And what agent doesn't need that?

If you ignore this advice, you'll be like the plumber who goes into someone's home to replace a section of pipe. You reach into your toolbag, but all you can find is a tiny screwdriver that won't even begin to correct the problem.

What are you going to get accomplished? Absolutely nothing.

PREPARE YOURSELF

The best way to prepare for the listing appointment is to get yourself ready mentally. Mental preparation can accomplish wonders.

Let's take the cases of two real estate agents about to embark on very similar listing appointments—same type of houses, same type of neighborhoods and same type of owners.

One of the agents would be thinking, "I'm going on this appointment, but I'll bet I don't get it. I haven't been doing very well lately when it comes to getting listings, so I probably won't get this one. And gee, that seller sounded awfully grouchy."

The other agent would be thinking, "I should get this one. I'm going to go out there and make all the preparations. I know they want to sell, and I'm really going to work hard at getting the listing. And if I don't get it right away, I'll keep trying."

On which of the two salespeople would you place your bets? The one with the positive mental attitude, surely.

While driving to your listing appointment, take along a cassette recorder. But instead of music (you're not going to dance when you get there), put on a motivational tape. Even a self-recorded tape of your own voice repeating, "I will get the listing, I will get the listing, I will get the listing" will help inspire you for the task ahead.

And for heaven's sake, don't turn on the news. What if you hear a report indicating that real estate sales are down because of a faltering economy?

Get positive! Get excited! Get the listing! Having the right attitude can make the difference!

Too many salespeople are very uncomfortable in the atmosphere of a listing appointment, possibly because they are in a stranger's home. Successful real estate agents know what they must do during the appointment. They have to warm up the seller, find out what the seller is trying to accomplish, stage a visual presentation, get an agreement on net price, close on the seller, cut through stalls, handle objections, tour the property and gather information.

These responsibilities contribute to an agent's nervousness and discomfort. The agent looks at them from an aerial view, so to speak, or all at once. It's like the patient who complained to his doctor, "It only hurts when I do this," to which the doctor sharply replies, "Well, don't do that!"

The same advice is good for real estate agents. Don't look at the big picture all at once. Take it one step at a time. Handling matters one at a time diminishes fears and self-doubts. And it makes you more efficient and competent, which should help make a seller feel good about listing with you.

FOUR STEPS TO LISTING

There arc four objectives an agent should want to accomplish during the listing appointment. Learn these four steps and you'll be well on your way to mastering one-stop listings.

1. *Get the seller to like you.* You can do everything else to the last detail, but if you skip this stage, it can all be for naught. It isn't necessary to stage a grand production to win the seller's admiration. It's the little things that make a person like you—warm personality, sincere manner, the fact you wiped your feet before coming inside of the seller's house. Remember, elephants don't bite; it's the little things that make a difference.

Dress appropriately. You don't have to wear $800 suits. Just make sure you're tastefully and neatly attired as well as groomed. Sure, you can't, and shouldn't, judge a book by its cover. But people do. And if they judge you accordingly, who loses? In a business situation, you do.

2. *Find out what they want.* Ask a lot of questions and find out the seller's wants, needs, likes, dislikes and motivations. Also, gather all the information about the property itself.

3. *Show them how to get what they want.* That's where you come in. If the seller gives you the listing, you can serve him.

4. *Ask them to make a decision.* If you don't ask them to decide, they will decide not to decide right away. Some people think tomorrow will be the best time to make a decision. But when it comes to listings, tomorrow may never come. And you don't want to waste your time today.

There is a simple way to remember this four-step process. Remember the word L-I-S-T.

"L" is for lead-in. Get them to like you, and take control.

"I" is for investigate. Gather all the facts.

"S" is for show and sell. Motivate the seller to do business for you.

"T" is for tie-down. Ask for the decision. Get a commitment from the seller.

That's it. It's simple. But it's important you take the steps in the proper sequence. If you start out all business, then try to warm up to the seller, the appointment won't flow as smoothly as you would like.

Let's go on an imaginary listing appointment, not only to review the basics, but also to master the fine points—the finishing touches designed to help accomplish each objective. No matter the personality of the seller, if you stay on track, you will be in control, and the odds of leaving with a listing will be increased.

LEAD-IN

Try to win the seller's admiration. And you can start by not running over the family Doberman when you pull your car into the driveway, even though you know the canine will take a chomp at you when you get out of your car.

You'll probably be nervous. Don't show it, though. Like the deodorant commercial says, "never let them see you sweat."

Now ring the doorbell. The door opens. Does the seller ever look gruff? At first glance, you decide you'd rather try to get a listing out of that unruly Doberman that greeted you on your arrival.

It really doesn't matter how the seller looks. Under any circumstances, show the seller a smile—a great, big one. If you don't smile, the seller's bad attitude might rub off on you. And if you're both grouchy, how far are you going to get? But if the seller is a grouch, and you're all smiles, one of three things is going to happen:

- The seller will start smiling with you.

- You eventually will get grouchy with the seller.

- You'll remain all smiles, and the seller will be all grouchy for the duration of the appointment.

Let's look at the possibilities. The first option is what you want, because two smiling people are going to get along and, consequently, increase your odds of getting the listing. The second option is what you definitely don't want. Sellers have the right to be grouches in their homes, but you don't. If you act grouchy, you may be asked to leave.

Never—NEVER—get into an argument with prospects. And should you find yourself embroiled in one, politely lose. You will anyway. If by no other way, the seller will send you home with a half-filled, unsigned listing agreement.

The third option is a distinct possibility. But a grouchy seller may still do business with you. Such people are just naturally disagreeable. Just keep your sunny side up. If you get the listing, it really shouldn't matter if the seller acts like Attila the Hun.

OFFER A COMPLIMENT

Pay the seller a compliment. Be careful how you do it, though. Always put the seller in the picture. If you say, "That's an awfully nice suit you're wearing," you are not complimenting the seller. Instead, you're complimenting the seller's tailor, and nobody cares what you think about the seller's tailor.

Get the seller into the picture by actually linking him or her to the compliment itself. For example, "What a nicely landscaped lawn! Did you do it yourself, or was it professionally done?" Or "This is a great color combination in the living room. Did you arrange it yourself, or was it done by an interior decorator?"

If you passed the state real estate exam, you're intelligent enough to find something in or around the home on which to compliment the seller. If nothing else, you can say the sellers has beautiful children (although I wouldn't ask if they were homemade or professionally done!).

GO TO THE KITCHEN

The next step is to take the sellers to the kitchen table. Don't sit down in the living room and don't go to the study. The kitchen table is where you want to be.

Studies show that the kitchen table is the place where most couples make major decisions. Generally, the lighting is better there than elsewhere in the house. You have a table upon which to write, instead of using a clipboard. And Mr. and Mrs. Seller will be just a few feet from you, instead of across the room.

Sometimes, though not often, you may have trouble getting the sellers into the kitchen. "Come on into the living room," they might say. "It's more comfortable."

If you wanted to be comfortable, you would have stayed at home. Instead, you want to get a listing, and odds are best that you'll get it if you can get them to the kitchen table.

Give the sellers a benefit of sitting at the kitchen table. You might say something like, "Well, the kitchen would be better because I've got some things I'd like to show you, and I'll need a table upon which to place them. I also will have some writing to do, and the lighting probably is much better in your kitchen."

If you saw the kitchen on your way inside the home, you might try this approach: "It seemed like a nice, warm room—real comfy, you know. I just thought it might be nice to sit there." Who knows? An approach like that could even get you a free dinner.

The point is, if you want to sit at the kitchen table, nine times out of ten, you can find a way to get there. And when you do, try to position each seller so both are facing you. You can make a much stronger presentation if you're facing them instead of having each seller at a different elbow.

MONEYMAKER NO. 1

By this time, you may have already met with opposition when Mr. Grouchy Seller says, "I'm not going to list tonight, so don't get your hopes up." Or, "We're not going to list until we talk to a few more brokers. So get on with your routine, but make it fast."

Don't let anything throw you off track. Instead, use a two-word phrase designed to keep you on track, no matter what the sellers says. I call this phrase "Moneymaker No. 1." Here it is—"No problem."

If a seller says, "No listings today," you come back with "No problem." Then head for the kitchen table.

This phrase even works on the telephone. Suppose you have telephoned a "for sale by owner," who says, "Wait a minute, I don't want to list my house." Just say, "No problem." Then get right back on track. "I would like to stop by and take a look at your house and leave you some information that will help you. . . ."

Get right back on track. After all, you're there to sell the sellers on the benefit of listing, and you must get your chance to do it. The seller still may not list with you, even after you've gone through all the necessary steps of a listing appointment. But at least there is a chance. If nothing else, you've done your best, and even if you're turned down, sellers always can change their minds later.

On the other hand, if you give up at the first objection, you'll have no chance of getting the listing. So play the odds, no matter how grouchy the seller seems (unless the seller grabs a shotgun or calls the Doberman).

WHO'S NERVOUS?

You're seated at the kitchen table with Mr. and Mrs. Seller. Are you nervous? Any time you get a chance to make $1,000 or so, you'd best be at least a little nervous, if nothing else but to get your adrenaline flowing. After all, you're the star of this show. And as any Broadway or Hollywood star will attest, when you lose the butterflies in your stomach before a performance, that's when it's time to quit. You never want to lose those butterflies; instead, you want them to fly in formation.

Are Mr. and Mrs. Seller nervous? Bet your commission on it. They are taking the preliminary steps to sell one home and to buy another. On a scale of one to ten of life's major purchases, you've got a good idea where this rates.

So here are three nervous people. What do you do? Start your sales pitch? You haven't finished with your lead-in. Just because you've said something nice about the sellers' front lawn and kitchen doesn't mean that the sellers like you yet.

Don't discuss real estate right away. Talk about anything else, such as baseball, hot dogs, cars, dogs, children, the weather, television . . . anything you can think of that you believe will get the sellers involved in a conversation with you.

Look for little tip-offs around the home that will help you find a topic. Maybe there are some trophies for golfing, bowling or other sports on display. Mention them. Perhaps there are needlepoint crafts hanging on the walls. Comment on them.

How do you know when the sellers start warming up to you? They start smiling more often, or their conversation flows more freely. They might tell you a joke, offer you some coffee or put away the Doberman. Until you see that the sellers are warming up to you, keep chatting about matters of universal concern. If you start your pitch before they're comfortable with you, it's going to be wasted.

That's why it doesn't pay to go into steps two, three and four until you've accomplished the first step, the lead-in. Smile, compliment and chat—at the kitchen table.

INVESTIGATE

Once a rapport with the sellers has been established, it's time to investigate. Gather all the facts. Find out the sellers' wants, needs, likes, dislikes and motives for moving. Do this by asking "wopen" questions. Those are open questions that start with the five Ws— who, what, when, where and why. They can't be answered with a "yes" or a "no." The seller must elaborate.

For example, "Where do you want to move?" "When do you want to move?" "Why do you want to move?" "What kind of a house are you looking for?"

No matter how many "wopen" questions you ask, or forget to ask, make sure that you ask this one: "Just out of curiosity, what would it take to get you to list with me tonight?"

I wouldn't kick-off the investigation phase of the appointment with that question. That would be a bit premature, especially if you had already been told that they didn't intend to list right away. But I also wouldn't want you to leave without at least asking that question at some point during the visit. After all, that's why you're there. If you don't ask for the listing, the sellers may give it to another real estate agent—one who knows how to ask the question.

First, you should get permission to ask questions. Without the sellers' permission, you'll be selling to inattentive prospects. They won't participate as you would like, and you'll be wasting your time. So you might say, "To best serve you and to provide you with the information you need, is it okay if I ask you some questions to learn your motivations for considering a sale?"

Most of the time, the sellers will agree. But even if they don't, use Moneymaker No. 1. Respond with "No problem," and proceed with more small talk until you feel like they have warmed up to you, or until they ask you to leave (which will be highly unlikely if they've agreed to let you visit in the first place).

Questions frighten a lot of agents. In fact, asking questions unnerves some agents to the point that they drop out of the business. They just have too much difficulty asking them.

But there is power in questions. The person asking them is usually in control, and the person answering them is most always interested. It's vitally important to keep in control and to keep the prospects interested. So it's equally important to learn how to ask questions.

It's easy to learn the right questions in a class situation. But sometimes, in the heat of an actual listing appointment, all those right questions seem to escape an agent somehow. So it would not be a bad idea to photocopy a list of appropriate questions, so you'll have a reference should your mind draw a blank during the interview.

GET THE SELLER TO AGREE

The opposite of "wopen" questions is "tie-down" questions, also known as commitment, or closing, questions. These must be answered with a "yes" or "no."

There is a belief that if you can prompt people to say "yes" to all the little questions that come up in a sales conversation, it will be much easier to elicit that big "YES" that you want. This is the "yes" that comes between "Will you list with me tonight?" and "Great! Here's the pen. Press hard, it's cheap carbon."

With that in mind, one way to bring this about is to ask a "wopen" question or two, then follow up with a tie-down question, such as, "To what area are you moving?" After the seller says, "We're going to the Happy Hollow subdivision," write down the answer, then ask a simple tie-down question like, "Gee, that's a nice area over there, isn't it?"

Understand the significance of the question. You are looking for agreement. And it would be difficult for the seller to disagree with a question such as this one. You're virtually guaranteed a "yes" because the sellers just told you they planned to move there. You would be quite surprised to hear them say, "Actually, no, it isn't a nice area. It looks like a slum to us, but we're going there to feel more at home, because we were reared in the ghetto."

The next question you may ask could be something like, "Aside from it being a nice neighborhood, is there any other reason you're considering moving over there?"

The seller may say, "Well, it's closer to my place of employment." Then you can come back with another tie-down question, such as, "Sounds like that will save you some time, am I right?"

Both examples are very safe tie-down questions. The seller practically answered them before you asked. So why ask them at all? You're conditioning the seller to say "yes." It's all part of salesmanship, showmanship or both. (The two are definitely close cousins, if not blood brothers.)

Aside from "wopen" and tie-down questions, there are also interest questions. They're good for finding out just how committed to selling the seller actually is. Suppose you're on an "expired listing" visit. You might ask the owner, "If I could show you why your home didn't sell and also that I could sell it by doing some things that the other broker didn't do, would you consider listing with me tonight?"

The worst the seller could do is refuse. And you know how to handle that. Refer to Moneymaker No. 1. "No problem." Then you get back on track.

Some of the questions agents ask of sellers also may be found on a standard listing agreement. And since you're going to write down the answers anyway, why not write them on the appropriate space on the listing agreement? You have one with you, remember? Thirty to fifty percent of it was filled out before you left the office. If it wasn't, you can definitely start filling it out at the seller's home.

This could be a bit intimidating to the sellers, especially if they're "for sale by owners" who already have said they don't plan to list. But that may be all right. It is part of the selling process.

Keep the listing agreement in plain sight early enough to get the seller accustomed to it. The worst thing the seller could do is say, "Hey, wait a minute. You don't have to fill that out because we're not going to list!"

And you know how to handle that. "No problem. Until it's signed, it's just a worksheet of no value to anyone but me. If you'd like, I'll leave a copy when I'm finished. How does that sound?"

TOUR THE HOME

If the sellers will permit it, take a tour of the house. This is the last scientific phase of the whole process. So use showmanship, and ask a lot of questions.

Get the seller to participate in measuring the rooms. This is good showmanship. It keeps the seller involved in the process, so when it's time to close, the seller may feel better about listing.

Which end of the tape measure do you hold? The beginning of it. That means the seller gets the measuring end. Why could it possibly matter? Suppose you are holding the measuring end while you and the seller measure the length of the living room. The seller asks how long it is, and you say, "Eighteen and a half feet." Then the seller asks, somewhat disappointingly, "Is that all?" The only thing you can say is, "That's right, that's all." And this will be a strike against you, because it will be as if you're the bearer of bad news.

But the other way, you can ask how long the room is. The seller will say, "Eighteen and a half feet," and then you can respond with, "Is that all?" This is good psychology, especially when it comes time to list. It gives the impression the seller may not have such a great house after all.

HOW TO TOUR

Have you ever seen a perfect home? They not only don't make them that way anymore, they never did. Any house standing today has a crack in the wall, a squeaky floor or some other defect that the buyer will find on a tour.

So while touring the home, use the "eyes" of a buyer, or you'll overestimate an asking price for the property. At the same time, you can't forget the seller's point of view. Otherwise, you'll under-price it, and the seller won't list.

And don't forget your own eyes. You also have to look at the house from your own point of view. When the home is sold, there is likely to be a mortgage, and the lender will want the real estate or marketing expert's opinion.

So don't get carried away by the defects. But it is a good idea to write down every one you see. This will serve as good conditioning for the seller when it comes time to list.

Suppose you take no note of defects. Instead, you rave about the positive features of the home. With every positive remark, an imaginary cash register bell is going off in the seller's head. If you remark enough about what a fine house it is, the seller may develop the courage to ask $100,000 for his $80,000 home.

Instead, take note of the negatives. You don't need to say any-thing. Just shake your head a little sadly when you find that squeak in the floor, write it down and move on. Who knows? If you find enough defects, the seller may beg you to list the rickety old shack. Maybe not. But you definitely will be strongly suggesting that the house is not perfect and will not bring a perfect price.

MONEYMAKER NO. 2

Here's another two-word phrase that can help you make money: "I would." When do you use it? Whenever a potential seller gives you the chance. Suppose the seller asked, "Do you think I should paint this room to help make the house sell?" How would you answer?

Some agents would try to be heroes. They might say, "Oh, don't bother, and we'll see what the other agents say." Or perhaps the seller wants to know if the refrigerator should be left behind. Some agents would say, "Well, we'll list it as optional, and maybe we can get you a few bucks for it."

The sellers ask these questions because they want to make their homes more salable. And all things being equal, a buyer will select the home which he or she feels offers the most for the money. In many cases, that will boil down to the house with the most gadgets or the freshest paint jobs.

So when a seller asks your advice on whether to leave behind the refrigerator, what are you going to say? That's right. "I would." Whenever advice is sought on such matters, simply say, "I would." And then write down the suggestions. Anything that the seller wants to do to make the home more salable can't help but ensure money into both of your pockets.

And getting money is why you're in this business, isn't it?

SHOW AND SELL

Take the sellers back to the kitchen table and show them the visuals you brought. Any material, printed or otherwise, that can help the sellers make a positive decision to list with you should be in your briefcase.

Always be on the lookout for such aids. It might take the form of a newspaper article stating that now is a good time to buy or sell a house. Clip it, laminate it and keep it in your briefcase, so you'll have it on hand to show to potential buyers and sellers.

Perhaps the seller has no confidence in real estate brokers, especially if the seller is an "expired listing." Show your credentials. If you've completed training courses, show them copies of the certificates. Better yet, show them testimonials to your competence. When you have a satisfied buyer and/or seller, ask them to write brief letters attesting to your skill in handling their transaction.

You must ask for testimonials or you'll never get them, even if your clients are truly pleased with your services. But satisfied customers generally will compliment you at some point. Then you'll have the perfect opportunity to say, "If you really feel that way, I'd appreciate it if you'd write a brief testimonial letter that I can show to future prospects who may question my competency."

If they're truly satisfied with your service, they'll be glad to help you. After all, you helped them. Sure, you got paid for it, but people pay for unsatisfactory services every day. If they didn't, every fast food chain in the United States would fold overnight.

Just remember that when it's time for you to show and sell, it's your "day in court." Or if you'd prefer, the curtain is up, the footlights are lit and the spotlight is shining on you.

Impress them. Visuals are one way to do it.

There are a lot of old-timers who fail to see the significance of visuals. "That's not traditional with us," they say. "We never did it before, why should we do it now?" Are they making so much money that they don't want any more? If they are, they don't need visuals. But if they aren't, I'd strongly recommend they use them. Visuals will increase your odds of getting a listing. And the more listings you have, the more commissions you'll get.

Of course, visual presentations can be awkward at first. But as you become acquainted to them, you'll be more comfortable and, as a result, more natural with them. And every time you use them, you'll improve until you reach the point where you can stage your presentation with your eyes closed.

TIE-DOWN

It's time for the heavy questions. You've asked enough agreement questions, and you've softened the seller a bit since your arrival. Now for the point of your visit. The heavy question you came to ask is, "What would it take for you to consider listing with me tonight?"

The sellers might say, "If we didn't have to pay a commission, we would list."

Sounds like there's no way out, doesn't it? There's always a way out. You could respond with, "So if I understand you correctly, you would list with me if you saw it wouldn't cost you any money, is that right?"

They just about have to agree, unless they just plain don't like you and are willing to tell you so. Then you point out to the sellers that, in all likelihood, listing with you will not only not cost them a cent, but actually could save them money.

If they are "for sale by owners," point out that there is a seventy percent chance they are wasting time, since seven out of ten eventually list with an agent. And time is money. They have but to look at rising prices and interest rates to determine that. So if the odds are strong that they will wind up paying a commission anyway, why wait?

Suppose you have a seller who hesitates to list because other agents have said they could get more than your recommended asking price. Prove to the seller that the only way one agent can get more for a house than another is if the lower price doesn't reflect the true market value. And with visuals such as a comparative market analysis and a multi-listings book, you should justify your price as just right for the market.

Agents don't sell houses. Houses sell houses. Agents find buyers. And tell the seller that you don't know of any agent who would work any harder to find a buyer than you.

It's called selling. And the more you "sell" yourself to the seller, the better your chances of getting the listing.

IN A CAPSULE

1. On a listing appointment, any possible objection that could arise probably will. Prepare for it by bringing along any publication or visual that could help you deal with them.

2. Get yourself mentally prepared before going on an appointment. A positive attitude is an asset, indeed, while a negative attitude can mentally cripple you.

3. Remember the key to listing, L-I-S-T: lead-in, investigate, show and sell and tie down. It's important that you take each step in its proper sequence. Get the seller to like you, find out what the seller wants, show how to get it and ask for a decision. It only works in that order.

4. During the lead-in phase, try to win the seller's admiration. Pay a compliment, and talk about anything except real estate. Prospects don't care how much you know, unless they know how much you care.

5. During the investigation phase, ask a lot of questions to determine the sellers' wants and needs. Use "wopen" questions, which begin with one of the five Ws—who, what, when, where and why. Then tour the home to get a feel for it. Get the seller to participate in the tour by helping you measure rooms.

6. During the show and sell phase, be sure to use visuals. Never tell prospects anything you can show them. Use company material, market analyses or expired listings.

7. During the tie-down phase, ask what it would take to get the listing. Show the prospects how they can benefit by listing with you.

8. Get the seller to agree with you by using tie-down questions. The more agreement you have on minor points, the easier it will be for prospects to agree on major points.

9. Remember the "Moneymakers." No. 1—"No problem." Use that whenever you get an objection. No. 2—"I would." Use that whenever a seller asks you whether to take certain steps to make a house salable. Don't talk yourself out of a commission.

List the most important points you have gained from the
preceding Strategy:

_____

_____

_____

_____

_____

_____

_____

_____

_____

_____

_____

_____

_____

_____

_____

_____

_____

_____

6

Make Your Listing Sell

I'll never forget my first boss in the real estate business. If Adolph Hitler ever had a brother in Michigan, I used to work for him. This man provided a stark contrast to the typical office manager we learned about in real estate school. They led us to believe that we would be cheered on when we came back with a listing.

Not my boss! We called him H. B. (for Hitler's Brother). We would try to sneak through the back door with our listings. But he would catch us and call us over to his desk. There, he would draw circles all over our listings with his red pen, having the audacity to show us the errors that we made!

I used to get so mad at him. He would actually force us to make money. I once told him, "You can't tell me what to do. I'm an independent contractor." And he said, "Fine, go contract somewhere else." That brought me down to earth really fast.

I can hear him talking now. "We're not going to list properties, spend our life servicing them, have them expire, let a co-broker re-list and make a commission.'' Then he would start circling deficiencies in our listings—right in front of us.

"Hey, Floyd, this house is overpriced by $8,000. You can't get away with that," H. B. would say. "Well, they won't come down $8,000," I'd reply. "No, but they'll come down $2,000 four times," he'd respond. Then he would circle the price.

"Hey, Floyd, what's this "ninety-day" listing? You know that's not enough time to sell a lot of houses. Two out of five homes take longer than ninety days to sell." Then he would circle the length of the listing.

"Hey, Floyd, what's this 'low commission'?" he asked. "Oh, they seemed like such nice people, H. B. And sometimes, commissions can be negotiable, can't they?" I'd say. "Sure, but it takes a minimum to run a business," he'd respond, "unless you want to make up the difference out of your own pocket."

And I'd say, "Circle it, H. B."

I always thought that H. B. was a tyrant. But he was only trying to teach us how to fend for ourselves and survive in the business. Consequently, there is one principle that H. B. instilled in me. And until you learn this, you'll do nothing but spin your wheels.

The principle? Worse than no listing at all is a listing that won't sell. And if the listing doesn't sell, what good is it? In fact, not only is it not good, it's downright bad. Energy spent on a listing that's doomed to expire is very time consuming, and, thus, costly to the agent, because time is money. It's very frustrating to the seller, and it hurts the real estate industry in general. No matter why the house didn't sell, the agent is going to be the villain.

Enough unsalable listings will ruin your reputation for that very reason. When asked why the house didn't sell, you don't expect the seller to say, "Well, I had it priced too high," or "My terms were ridiculous." No, the seller is going to say, "The agent had neither the gumption nor the sense to sell my house."

This chapter will detail many of the reasons why some listings don't sell. And it will also include pointers on how to make listings salable. The main philosophy behind this chapter is the fact that both agent and seller have responsibilities. The seller must do whatever is necessary to make the house salable. It's the agent's responsibility to make sure the seller knows just what to do.

Multi-million-dollar producers adopt an attitude of "I don't work miracles. The seller has to do his or her share. I can only do my part." And if the seller refuses to do what is necessary, the multi-million-dollar producer lets the seller find another agent. Multi-million-dollar producers let the competition get stuck with unsalable listings. They don't need them.

THE RIGHT PRICE

There are three prices for a home—the wholesale price, the retail price and the seller's price. The first two are pretty clear. You can find out about them through market analyses and similar listings. But agent and seller will likely disagree on the asking price. After all, the seller often has an inflated opinion of the house's value. Just because a seller insists on getting $82,000 for his $75,000 home doesn't mean the agent must take the listing.

No amount of selling in the world can sell houses people don't want to buy. And asking $7,000 more than a house is worth is a good way to turn off prospective buyers. If you take such a listing, it may expire. And you will have indirectly helped another agent get a commission, because when the seller re-lists, it won't be with you.

If you can't get the price down to a reasonable level, it might be better to refuse the listing and let the seller harass one of your competitors. But you'll be better off to find a method for establishing a price for a house that will make both seller and buyer (and, of course, yourself) happy.

THREE FACTORS FOR SALABLE LISTINGS

When you go on a listing appointment, remember that there are three important factors in making listings salable—price, terms and the seller's motivation to relocate.

The first ingredient is price. Many sellers think price is the most important thing. You'll find they will offer a great deal of resistance if you ask them to consider lowering their prices. Consequently, many agents may think that if they can't list the house at the right price, they should just not list it at all. But that's acting a bit hastily. Price is only one of three components of a salable listing.

The second component is terms. An overpriced listing could sell tomorrow for $50,000 more than the listed price—provided the seller would accept ridiculous terms, such as a dollar down and a dollar per month at one percent interest. This example is, of course, highly unrealistic, but it illustrates the point. If you can't get the right price for the house, try for the right terms. A competitive interest rate or a competitive down payment could be positive factors to attract a buyer.

The third factor is motivation of the seller to relocate. If the seller is ready to move right away, you might accept the listing, even if the price and terms are a bit out of line. Suppose the seller is motivated to make a move within ninety days because of a transfer to another city or a voluntary career change. Even if price and terms are unreasonable, take the listing.

Why would you want to do that? As the time for the seller's scheduled move approaches and the house hasn't sold, you'll have a great argument for lowering the price and/or terms. The fact that the seller must move by a certain date could be a beautiful door-opener for you to get a price adjustment.

Of course, you know what a price adjustment is. Actually, it's lowering the price. You wouldn't want to raise the price of a house half-way through the listing period, unless you learned that the President of the United States had just purchased the house next door with plans to move in once he moves out of the White House.

So if price and terms are unreasonable, and the seller is in no hurry to move, you should definitely refuse the listing. But if the opposite is true in only one of these factors, take the listing. But if the price is a bit high, the market may catch up within the next six months.

COMPARE WITH OTHER HOMES

One of the best ways to set a price for a house is by determining the price of other comparable homes in the market area that have recently sold. Price ranges fluctuate from low to high. Suppose you're looking at a home similar to those that have recently sold for between $80,000 and $90,000. There's a range of low to high. What range will the seller select? The seller always favors the high range. And many times, so does the agent on the assumption that the listing will otherwise be lost.

But there are times when an agent should recommend the low part of the range, depending upon several factors.

1. *Seller's motivation to relocate.* The seller may be getting a new position, a transfer or a divorce. Or the seller may have already found a new home and is ready to move into it right away. For whatever reason, if the

seller needs a fast sale, then pricing the home toward the low end of the range will help make it attractive to buyers.

2. *Difficult terms.* Suppose the owner's house is located in an FHA or VA or other government financing area. The owner wants to sell the home at other than government financing terms. Perhaps the owner is worried about paying points or making repairs. A home can be sold under stringent terms, provided the house is listed on the market at a sufficiently low price, offering the buyer a bargain.

3. *Poor condition.* Suppose the home is in need of extensive repair. That doesn't mean it won't sell; the world is filled with people interested in restoring old houses. But they're not going to pay top dollar for them. It's your job to communicate to the seller the benefits of putting such properties on the market at the low end of the range. The lower the price, in most cases, the more certain the sale.

But there are times when the higher part of the range is preferred. And if the higher range is warranted, that's great. After all, the higher the price, the higher your commission and the happier your seller is going to be.

There are four factors that justify pricing toward the high end—slow sale, seller unmotivated to relocate, easy terms and excellent condition.

1. *Slow sale.* Suppose you are dealing with a seller who owns a nice home but is planning to retire in six months to another part of the country. In short, the seller wants to unload the home but remain in it until the retirement date.

This is a good time to overprice a home. In such cases, homes priced toward the high end generally take several months to sell. By the time they actually sell, the market may have caught up with the price, making it a fair one, indeed. And should the house sell right away, the agent and seller could agree to cut several thousand dollars from the price in exchange for extended occupancy for the seller.

In this case, the seller could end up with a greater net in his pocket. And so could you. Or the seller could take the time and get the right price for the house.

2. *Seller unmotivated to move.* This is the seller who would gladly put his or her home on the market if you could find that century-old, completely remodeled farmhouse located on twenty acres just outside the city. In such a case, you might as well price the home on the high end, because there is no motivation to sell (and possibly no desire) unless you find the specific house. If you do, you've got room for a price reduction on the present home to help speed up the sale.

3. *Easy terms.* Should you forget about acquiring a listing if the seller wants more than the house is worth? Not if you can get easy terms. If you can convince the seller to settle for a sufficiently low down payment, or to hold the mortgage and finance the sale, you can possibly motivate a buyer into paying more for the home.

4. *Excellent condition.* You can get away with a high-end price if the seller's home is in excellent condition. In the real estate business, such homes are called "cream puffs."

USE A COMPARATIVE MARKET ANALYSIS

Pricing is not scientific. It's based upon logic. That's why you should have a thorough knowledge of what price comparable homes are selling for in your market.

Get access to a comparative market analysis, or a CMA, as it's commonly called. It's a guide that generally consists of three sections—a listing of homes which have recently sold in the area, a listing of homes which currently are available and a collection of homes with listings that have expired.

Suppose you're appraising what is commonly known as a standard, one-story brick home. It has three bedrooms, a family room and an attached garage. You won't find any home exactly like the one you're trying to sell. Why? There are no two homes exactly alike. Every home is different. You may not think so, but you can rest assured that the seller will think his or her house is unique.

The best you can do is to compare types of homes with others on the market. Suppose you find a house matching the description of the one you want to list, except that it doesn't have a family room, or an attached garage, or it has one less bedroom than the other. Then you can make your adjustments accordingly.

Knowing what other homes have sold for will help you set the price for the seller's property. The property you are appraising will sell only at one price, and that's the price the buyer is willing to pay for it. And the most reliable facts on hand to determine this price is what others have paid for similar properties in your market area.

The most current information about property prices can be obtained through the CMA. It's important that the sellers understand their competition. If all other comparable homes are listed on the current market at $85,000, the seller may price the home out of the market by asking for $92,000. The CMA is the best method of obtaining appropriate facts applicable to the particular homes that you are trying to list. In some cases, you may only find one home that is comparable to the house you're trying to list. In other cases, you may find a half dozen or more.

KEEP PRICING SIMPLE

When you're talking with prospective buyers, you only have one responsibility—to share with them some facts and then make a proposal on the price of the net profit a sale would bring.

It's important that you make a proposal. This places the proverbial ball in the seller's court. He or she may either accept or reject your proposal. If he or she rejects, he or she may make a counter proposal. But if you start off the pricing process by asking what the seller wants for the home, the seller will go for the high end every time.

When you put the ball in the seller's court, he or she must at least return it to you by either accepting or rejecting your proposal. If the seller accepts, the ball is back in your court. Take the listing and run.

On the other hand, let's say you've proposed a price of $85,000, but the seller wants to stick with $90,000. You must make the decision. Will you list at $90,000, or do you make a counter proposal?

If you opt for a counter-proposal, you might try it this way:

"Mr. and Mrs. Woochkowski, let's just pretend that I couldn't get you $90,000 because, based on the market analysis and the facts I have, I probably won't be able to get it. Let's just say that the best I could get would be $87,000. Would you take it?"

The ball has been returned to the seller's court. And the two of you can bounce it back and forth until the price is established.

GET THE LISTING RIGHT

I once knew an agent who won an award one year for getting the most listings of all agents in a particular market area. The agent was proud, the broker was proud and everyone at the award ceremony was applauding, thinking about what a hard worker the agent was. But after doing some investigation, I learned that only fifteen percent of those listings actually sold. That means the agent was breaking his back to make an income below the poverty level.

Why do some listings sell and some don't? As I said earlier, it's often because of major factors like price and/or terms. But even a satisfactory price and good terms won't guarantee the sale of a home. There are many little things that must be taken into consideration.

Obviously, price and terms are important. But they alone don't make a listing (although they can certainly break it). Remember that airplane checklist we talked about earlier? Let me offer such a list to use for obtaining a successful listing. Just as the airplane checklist is designed to help assure a successful trip, this checklist is designed to obtain a listing that will sell.

There are twenty points to be applied. Unlike the airplane checklist, there's a little leeway with this list. Studies show that if a seller agrees to at least eleven or twelve of the points, odds are you'll have a successful salable listing.

Even if the seller won't budge on certain points, there is still room for a successful listing, as long as the seller will be reasonable on others. And it's vitally important for you to get the listings right. You need a strong inventory of salable houses, and a property listed properly is half sold at the beginning.

SALABILITY CHECKLIST

A salability checklist can accomplish several valuable objectives. It can:

- Offer a viable form of communication between salesperson and management when reviewing listings.

- Serve as a standards list for the agent.

- Put the "monkey" on the seller's back. The seller must do his or her part. Agents can't and shouldn't try to work miracles.

- Be a good prospecting tool for "expired listings." Ask such homeowners if the former agent used the checklist for the previous listing. If not, you can explain what it is in terms designed to impress the prospect.

When listing a home, try to get the seller to agree on as many of the following points as possible. The more points to which the seller agrees, the more certain the eventual sale of the home.

1. *List home between wholesale and retail price based on how much time there is before the seller wants the cash out of the sale.* Determine that price by using the "pyramid structure."

    For example, let's say the home you want to list is valued at $80,000. But the house must be sold immediately. Chances are excellent the seller won't get anywhere near the full market value. In fact, experience shows that to sell a house immediately, the price should be seventy to seventy-five percent of the market price and sold outright to an investor (or buy it). In this case, you should sell (or buy) this $80,000 house at $56,000 to $60,000.

Use the "pyramid structure" to determine the asking price for a house. Imagine a pyramid. It starts small and gradually widens to a full-sized base. This concept is good to determine an asking price. The sooner the seller wants the cash, the lower the asking price should be.

Immediate move—
70%
One to two months—
80%
Two to three months—
85%
Three to four months—
90%
Four to five months—
95%
Six months or more—
100%

Suppose the seller has one to two months before moving. You would refer to the pyramid structure (on Page 117) and determine that the asking price must be eighty percent of the full market value. In this case, it will be $64,000. Suppose the seller's new home will be ready in three to four months. Then, the seller will need the cash out of the present home. By referring to the pyramid structure, the price should be set at ninety percent of the asking price, or $72,000. Of course, these examples are only hypothetical. But keep in mind the pricing process, and make it work for you.

2. *Always try to list the house at an odd price.* Instead of listing it at $72,000, try $71,800. What difference

COMPLETE MARKET & PROCESSING TIME

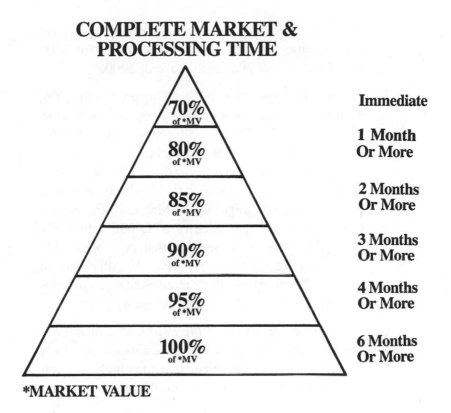

70% of *MV — Immediate

80% of *MV — 1 Month Or More

85% of *MV — 2 Months Or More

90% of *MV — 3 Months Or More

95% of *MV — 4 Months Or More

100% of *MV — 6 Months Or More

*MARKET VALUE

could $200 make? Plenty, when it comes to the multi-listings book. This publication consists of scores of homes in your market area, positioned in the book in order of ascending price.

Most home buyers start looking in the low price ranges and work upward until finding the suitable house. A house priced at $71,000 may be located as many as three pages in the multi-listings book before a house listed at $72,000.

117

What a shame it would be if your home was never seen because a seller found a suitable one for $200 less! Don't lose a sale for the love of $200.

3. *Pre-condition the seller.* If the asking price is $75,000, what do you suppose the seller's reaction will be to an offer of $70,000? The seller may refuse an offer that's $5,000 below what he sought.

   If you condition the seller early to consider a lower price, it can improve the chances of selling the house. For example, you might say, "Mr. and Mrs. Seller, would you consider a price of $72,000? I think it's likely that offers will range in that neighborhood." Then, if someone offers $70,000, the offer will be only $2,000 off in the seller's mind. And that's psychologically better than $5,000 below asking price.

4. *Pre-order an appraisal of the house.* If it runs lower than the asking price, you will have a means of getting the seller to lower the price. If it runs higher, you'll have a good tool to motivate the buyer to purchase.

5. *If the seller is financing the house, list a competitive down payment from zero to fifteen percent.* This will attract buyers, even those who might ordinarily object to paying full price. Sometimes, price isn't the most important factor in buying a house. If the terms are easy enough, full price may be no problem.

6. *Shoot for a competitive interest rate, provided the seller is willing to finance the house.* Find out how low the seller will go. If necessary, stress that the seller must sacrifice to make the house attractive to buyers. At the same time, you may also stress that you are indeed on the seller's side. After all, the better the price the house will bring, the better your commission. But if the house doesn't sell, both you and the seller will

lose. A buyer simply will not be motivated to purchase if there is no apparent advantage.

7. ***Wherever and whenever possible, list the house for government terms, such as FHA and VA.*** Eliminating those terms reduces the prospective pool of buyers, and that increases the odds of not selling the home.

8. ***If a fast sale is important, perhaps the seller would consider an eight percent commission, rather than the standard six percent.*** The higher commission certainly would inspire agents to sell because of the extra financial incentive. An extra percentage of commission is especially good motivation when the real estate market is tight and sales are down. After all, the fewer houses that are sold, the fewer your chances of having your listings sold.

9. ***If possible, list the house with trade-in terms.*** This wouldn't be applicable if the seller is moving to another state. But if the seller is relocating across town, a trade might be possible. Perhaps the seller wants a larger home, and a prospective buyer might have one that would be suitable. It's not unusual for an older couple to scale down to a smaller home once the children are grown and gone.

10. ***Word your listings carefully to attract the reader's attention.*** Use phrases, if applicable, such as "low interest," "immediate possession," and "closing costs move you in."

11. ***List for a minimum of one-hundred-eighty days.*** This cuts down on expired listings. Two out of every five homes take longer than ninety days to sell. Yet, many real estate agencies list homes for only ninety days. That means that forty percent of the time, a ninety-

day listing is doomed to fail. A longer listing also will allow the seller to set the price above the norm, and the market may catch up with the price during the six-month period.

12. *Offer immediate possession.* By advertising immediate possession, potential buyers will have greater motivation to tour the property. With the proper listing period and an above average price, the seller can bargain with a buyer by accepting a lower price in exchange for extended occupancy of the house.

13. *Allow buyers easy access to the house.* Access must not be restricted if the seller wants the house sold. Some sellers actually include in their listings "Sunday, 2-4 P.M. only." Or they only permit showings accompanied by a listing agent. Such stipulations sharply decrease the chances of selling a house.

There are three ingredients for a successful sale— a house, a seller and a buyer. All three must get together at the right time. If showings are restricted to certain days, or certain hours, the odds of combining the ingredients to make the sale will be decreased substantially.

And put the seller's telephone number in the listing. Some agents don't do this because they don't want to give away information that another agent could use to get a relist if their listing should expire. If that's the way you think, you have a defeatist attitude, and you should turn back to chapter one and read again about the importance of a positive attitude.

14. *Have the seller redecorate the house in the buyer's choice of colors.* If necessary, the sale price can be adjusted to accommodate the costs. It's no big deal.

15. ***Try to persuade the seller to include the extras.*** If the buyer offers a lower price, you can exclude the items or talk the seller into leaving them anyway. Remember, the more you can offer, the better your chances of attracting buyers.

16. ***Get a home protection insurance plan.*** It's a terrific listing tool. Many agents have them and don't use them. Either include the plan automatically or talk the seller into raising the price of the house accordingly. At worst, the seller has spent about $300. At best, the seller is covered if the furnace explodes.

17. ***Post a yard sign.*** When sellers refuse to do that, convince them that yard signs attract attention, and some people actually buy after seeing a sign. Tell the seller that, without a yard sign, the house could be the city's best kept secret. Some sellers say they don't want a sign because they don't want neighbors to know they are moving. But unless they plan to load the van at midnight, the neighbors are going to find out anyway.

18. ***Avoid contingencies.*** Stay away from listings which specify that a sale would depend upon other factors, such as the sale of an existing home. You don't need to be tied down to factors beyond your control.

19. ***Avoid panic phrases, such as "owner anxious" or "owner must sell."*** Of course, the owner must sell. There wouldn't be a listing if the owner didn't have to sell. Not only do such phrases tip the buyer that something is wrong, they also waste valuable selling space. Save it for comments about the home's features and benefits.

20. ***Make the house available for the next tour or caravan.*** Real estate companies often stage tours of available

homes. Agents can see what's on the market and line
up prospects for sales. If a house is included in a tour,
the odds of selling it will increase.

Go over this checklist when you're on a listing call. If at least
eleven or twelve of these points apply, chances are good that the
house will sell. Convince the seller to adopt as many of these principles
as possible. The sooner the house sells, the happier both of you
will be.

More than likely, a seller won't consent to all of these points.
The seller may insist on full market value, or the seller may demand
a twenty percent down payment. The seller may not list for FHA
or VA terms, or he or she may not even consider offering immediate
possession.

Whether to take the listing is up to you. If the seller is too
unreasonable, you may refuse it. Remember, if it won't sell, you
don't want it.

INSIST ON ONE-HUNDRED-EIGHTY DAYS

If you insist on any point, I hope it will be tip number eleven—
list the home for a minimum of one-hundred-eighty days. Tradition-
ally, in many areas, homes are listed for a maximum of ninety
days. There is no law to that effect. Somewhere in time, some
attorney probably stipulated that a house be listed for ninety days,
and real estate agents merely accepted that as the standard.

But ninety days isn't enough for forty percent of the listings.
That means that four times out of ten, the listing will expire, the
homeowner will be angry because the house wasn't sold, a competitor
will get the re-listing and you will lose the sale. In other words,
with a ninety-day listing, you just may be wasting your time.

To list a home for one-hundred-eighty days, try these proven methods:

1. Put one-hundred-eighty days in the listing agreement and say nothing. Most of the time, nothing more will be said, and the house will list for six months.

2. If the seller does ask the length of the listing period, simply reply, "One-hundred-eighty days" without flinching or wiggling. Don't show discomfort. Act as if one-hundred-eighty days is the norm.

3. In the event of protest, show the seller the area average is one-hundred-eighty days to sell a house. Tell the seller that if you were going to drive across the desert and you knew it took one-hundred-five gallons of gas to make the trip, you definitely wouldn't set out with just ninety gallons.

Of course, it really depends on how strongly you feel about it. I talked with one agent who was told by a potential lister that under no circumstances would the house list for one-hundred-eighty days. The agent calmly, but firmly, replied, "I'll not take the listing if I can't have one-hundred-eighty days."

You know what the agent got? One-hundred-eighty days.

Some agents have a different approach. They'll agree to anything, as long as the seller signs the listing agreement. Once that's done, then the agent will turn up the heat on the seller by saying, "You know, it really frustrates me that you won't include a yard sign, because that improves the chances of selling the house." Or, "It really frustrates me that you won't make your home more accessible to buyers and other agents, because you're greatly reducing the chances of selling it."

That's the back-door approach. If it works, it's fine. You must size up your seller. Some sellers won't care how frustrated you are. If you deal with them, it will be on their terms only. And terms such as theirs can cripple the possibility of a sale.

But if the seller will agree to most of the points of the Salability Checklist, it's likely that the home will be sold. Then, both you and the seller should be satisfied.

IN A CAPSULE

1. Worse than no listing at all is a listing that won't sell. Avoid taking unsalable listings.

2. There are three factors for a salable listing. The right price, the right terms and a highly motivated seller to relocate. If none of the factors are present, reject the listing. But if only one is present, you might still accept the listing.

3. Find the right price for a home by comparing with other similar homes in the area that have recently sold.

4. Recommend the low part of the price range if the seller is in a hurry to move or demands difficult terms. If the home is in poor condition, go with the lower price.

5. Recommend the high part of the price range if the seller wants a slow sale, is in no hurry to move or offers easy terms. If the house is in excellent condition, go with the higher price.

6. Use a comparative market analysis to sell the seller on accepting your recommended price.

7. Keep pricing simple. Make a proposal. If the seller objects, allow the seller to counter-propose. If you object, make another proposal. Treat the process as if it were a ping-pong game.

8. Get the listing right. Take a copy of the Salability Checklist on your listing appointment. If a listing is designed to coincide with most of the twenty points, it will be likely to sell.

9. Insist on listing the house for no less than one-hundred-eighty days. Two out of five homes take longer than ninety days to sell. Don't set yourself up for an expired listing.

List the most important points you have gained from the
preceding Strategy:

_____

_____

_____

_____

_____

_____

_____

_____

_____

_____

_____

_____

_____

_____

_____

_____

NOTES

Section 3

COURTING THE BUYER

7

Attract the Ad Caller

$\mathbf{A}$ man on a business trip telephoned home to speak with his wife. But the maid answered and said his wife was in her bedroom having an affair with his best friend.

Naturally, this infuriated the man. But being a thousand miles away, he was unable to take personal action. So instead, he persuaded the maid to act for him.

"I want you to go to the hall closet, where I keep my shotgun," the man ordered. "Get it, and kill both of them!"

"I can't do that," the maid protested.

"You will if you want to keep your job," the man responded.

The man listened on his end of the line and heard the maid walk to the hall closet, then up the stairs to the bedroom. Then he heard two shotgun blasts. After that, he heard the sounds of bodies being dragged across the floor, down the stairs and, finally, out the back door.

Several minutes later, the maid returned to the telephone and told her boss that she had done what he had asked.

"What did you do with the bodies?" the man asked.

"I threw them into the swimming pool," the maid replied.

"Swimming pool?!" the man exclaimed. "We don't have any. . . . Say, is this 273–5746?"

The man was indeed effective at persuasive communication. Unfortunately, he didn't really know with whom he was speaking.

This reminds me of some real estate agents. They'll get a call, talk a while, then hang up and say, "I'll tell you, that caller didn't hear a word I said." Or, "Boy, was that caller obnoxious?"

What they actually were saying was, "I didn't accomplish what I wanted." And do you know why? It's because, like the angry man, they didn't really know with whom they were talking.

If those agents fully realized that, "Hey, here is someone who might have $1,000 to give me," don't you think they would have made a better effort to communicate?

IDENTIFY YOUR CALLER

Know how to talk with a caller. What you say and how you say it is most important in regard to what finally happens. Don't invest a great deal of time with callers who are just looking. This is time that could be better spent by showing homes to potential buyers. Find out early if the caller is a qualified prospect. Odds are good that the caller is a serious buyer. Studies show that more than half of the people who call a real estate office will buy a house within ninety days. Unfortunately, they don't always buy from you. Many times, they go to the competition.

It's like a race. Races generally are won or lost right at the beginning. Too many salespeople lose prospective buyers right at the beginning by saying the wrong thing. Many times, an agent loses simply by giving away the address for the listing. Once that is done, callers usually don't want to talk anymore and they'll hang up. But will they call back? Not likely, because studies show that ninety-five percent of ad callers never buy the house that prompted them to call. When agents give out addresses, they can almost count on sending potential buyers to homes they won't buy.

Too often, salespeople make basic mistakes. They don't get enough information, or they give away too much information. They don't keep control of a situation, they don't get a telephone number or they don't have the prospect's best interest in mind. The bottom line is, they don't get the appointment.

Sometimes, it's a matter of attitude. There are salespeople who act like they're inconvenienced when the telephone rings, interrupting a conversation they're having with a co-worker or some other activity that could easily wait until later. They act as if answering the phone is a burden. They don't think that at least one of every two callers will buy a home within the next three months. They don't think that at least one of every two callers might be in a position to hand them $1,000 or more.

DEVELOP THE RIGHT ATTITUDE

Next time you're responsible for answering telephone calls, arrive early and get prepared. Load your "guns." Get all the information together. Know which ads are being displayed, have a copy of all your listings handy, in case you get a call as a result of a yard sign.

And repeat this to yourself whenever you have time: "Each caller has $1,000 of my money, and I want it." That may seem a bit silly. But agents who think in terms of profit will be more enthusiastic about motivating callers to come into their offices.

That's really the only thing an agent can accomplish on the telephone. Agents can't sell houses over it. Perhaps you know an agent who has done it once, maybe even twice. But those were isolated situations. Any real estate agent will tell you such cases are the exception, not the rule.

The only way to get callers into the office is by communicating with them. And communication occurs when a speaker can make another person understand a given point from the speaker's point of view.

FOUR STEPS TO GOOD COMMUNICATION

There are four components of effective communication, experts say. There must be:

1. A sender of the message.

2. A message to send.

3. A method for sending the message.

4. A receiver of the message.

Agents are the senders of the message. Handling the ad call is their responsibility, not the caller's. The objective is to get the receivers of the message, the callers, to understand the message from the agent's point of view.

What do agents have to communicate? Do they want to tell the caller that they're professionals? That's not good enough. That they can help? Still not good enough. That they have good selections of homes? Close, but still off target.

The message shouldn't be confused with the method. The message can only be one thing—come into the office, or CITO in real estate jargon. There's no other message an agent should want to communicate. Any other message can result in the loss of a lot of sales.

Some agents want to impress upon callers that they are professionals, but that won't entice callers to come into the office. Some agents talk about their large inventories, but that's no real drawing card, either.

What would motivate you to go anywhere? A message that appeals to you on your own terms. Prospective buyers must be told something they want to hear. Remember, they are considering a home purchase for their own reasons, not so an agent can make $1,000. Agents who can appeal to buyers on their own terms can increase their odds of selling houses.

FIRST CALL TOWARD COMMISSION

To illustrate my point well, take a look at the following transcript of a telephone conversation between a real estate agent and a prospective buyer who calls the agent after seeing an ad for a particular house in the local newspaper. After the transcript, we'll discuss how the agent handled the call.

AGENT: Good afternoon, On Track Realty, may I help you?

BUYER: I just wanted some information on a house I saw advertised.

AGENT: Thank you for calling. By the way, we advertise in several newspapers. In which newspaper did you see our ad?

BUYER: The News.

AGENT: And so I don't make a mistake, would you describe the ad to me?

BUYER: It starts with, "Closing costs move you in . . ."

AGENT: I see. Yes, I'd be happy to get that information. May I ask you to hold just a moment, please? . . . Thank you. Oh I'm sorry. My name is _____. What's yours?

BUYER: Gordon Freeland.

AGENT: Gordon Freeland. That's like "free land," isn't it? Okay, Mr. Freeland, what was it about that ad that caught your attention?

BUYER: I've been looking for an untraditional home.

AGENT: How long have you been looking for a home?

BUYER: About two months.

AGENT: Have you worked with any brokers at all?

BUYER: No, we don't really want to work with a broker until we find what we're looking for.

AGENT: Have you looked at many houses?

BUYER: A couple.

AGENT: Of the houses you've seen, what was it about them that you didn't like?

BUYER: Well, the rooms were too small.

AGENT: Okay, I've got the information I need now. What can I tell you about the home?

BUYER: What's the address?

AGENT: Well, I'd be happy to give you the address, but studies show that, if I do, you'd only be wasting time and gas. Most people don't buy the home they see advertised. Instead of possibly wasting your time, let me give you some information about the property, and then we'll talk about the address later. Fair enough?

BUYER: All right. What area is it in?

AGENT: It's in the Happy Hollow area. Are you familiar with that?

BUYER: Yes, I am. How many bedrooms does it have?

AGENT: It's got three bedrooms. Is that what you're looking for?

BUYER: Something along those lines, yes. How much do they want for it?

AGENT: They want $94,500. Were you thinking of investing more?

BUYER: Well, we're not certain at this time. Does it have a family room?

AGENT: Sure does. Could you use one of those?

BUYER: Most definitely. How about a fireplace?

AGENT: It has that, too. Does your current home have one?

BUYER: Yes. Is the home located near a school?

AGENT: In my opinion, it is. But you may not think so. What do you consider to be close?

BUYER: Within four or five blocks.

AGENT: It's close, then. What else can I tell you about the property?

BUYER: What size is the living room?

AGENT: I can't vouch for the accuracy, but according to our information, it's eighteen by fourteen feet. Does that sound large enough for you?

BUYER: That would be larger than the one we have now.

AGENT: Okay, what else can I tell you about it?

BUYER: What style would you say the home is?

AGENT: This particular one is a Cape Cod style. It's basically a one and three-quarter story home. Are you familiar with Cape Cod style?

BUYER: Yes, I am. How many bathrooms does it have?

AGENT: This one has two and one-half bathrooms. How does that sound to you?

BUYER: That would be fine. Do you think the owner would take any less than $94,500?

AGENT: Well, I'm not. . . . By the way, just in case, what is your phone number there, Gordon?

BUYER: 684–1010.

AGENT: Okay. Well, I'm not sure about whether the owner would take less. That's entirely between you and the owner. But Gordon, let me stop you for a moment, because I just had an idea I'd like to share with you, if I may.

BUYER: Sure.

AGENT: You said something earlier, Gordon, that just sparked a thought in my mind. And I believe you may have a minor problem working against you. May I share with you what I mean?

BUYER: Certainly.

AGENT: Okay. You mentioned that you're looking for an untraditional home, is that correct?

BUYER: That's right.

AGENT: Something with a unique appearance to it, right?

BUYER: Right.

AGENT: Okay, and you also mentioned that you've been looking for this home for two months. Did I hear you correctly?

BUYER: You did.

AGENT: Okay. Here's the potential problem, Gordon. It seems like you're looking for a special type of home. And it sounds like it even might be special enough that once it reaches the market, it may sell quickly. Thus, it may never reach the newspapers. Could that be a possibility?

BUYER: You'd probably know better than I would.

AGENT: All right. I have a solution to your problem. Have you ever heard of the multi-lists organization, Gordon?

BUYER: What's that?

AGENT: Through the multi-lists, I have access to virtually every home available anywhere in the area. I also have a current list of all new listings that come on the market. If we could possibly get together, I could get to know you a little bit, analyze your wants and needs and, perhaps, even show you a couple of homes. By learning your likes and dislikes, when your home does come on the market, you'll be the second one to know about it, because I'll be the first. Does that make sense to you, Gordon?

BUYER: Why, yes it does.

AGENT: Okay, could you stop by tomorrow after work, or would Thursday be better?

BUYER: Tomorrow's booked for me. But I definitely could make it Thursday.

AGENT: Thursday, it is. How about five P.M., or is that too early?

BUYER: That's a bit early. What about seven?

AGENT: Fine, Gordon. We're at 123 Main Street. Perhaps I will do a little bit of homework before you come, and I'll have some possibilities lined up. And if we don't accomplish any more than this on Thursday, at least we'll get to know each other. But I think I can find you the home you want.

BUYER: That sounds good to me.

AGENT: Okay, I thank you very much for calling, and I'll see you at seven P.M. Thursday.

The way the agent handled the call was absolutely, irrevocably scientific. The agent knew every step of the track (the step-by-step plan to achieve the objective). Because of that, the agent knew exactly what to say and when to say it—regardless of what the caller said. That's the beauty of tracks. An agent is prepared for anything, except for a bomb threat.

LOOKING DEEPER

Let's break down every segment of the conversation so you'll know how the agent determined what to say and when to say it.

"Good afternoon, On Track Realty, may I help you?"

Why didn't the agent just say, "On Track Realty" and let it go at that? Simple. There are only a few seconds to make a first impression. Agents might as well use them to their best advantage.

The caller asks about information on a house. The agent responded by saying, "Thank you for calling. By the way, we advertise in several newspapers. In which newspaper did you see our ad?"

This is called the "gratiscribe—a combination of gratitude and describe. The agent showed gratitude by thanking the caller. Then the agent asked for a description of the medium through which the caller became aware of the listing.

No matter what the caller says, the gratiscribe works. Suppose the caller was hostile and said, "I saw your ad in the paper and I want to get the information. If you don't want to give me the address, I'll just call some other agent."

The agent can still respond with the gratiscribe. It makes perfect sense. But most importantly, the agent maintains control of the conversation.

After the caller gives the name of the newspaper, the agent said, "And so I don't make a mistake, would you describe the ad to me?" This strengthens the agent's control of the conversation. Then the agent responds by saying, "I'd be happy to get you that information. May I ask you to hold just a moment, please?"

That's called the "offer and hold." Notice that the buyer gave the agent some information on the ad, and the agent responded with a good positive exclamation—"I'd be happy to get you that information." But before going on hold, the agent apologized for not giving his name, introduced himself and asked the caller's name. The agent did this rather matter of factly, as if it were almost a side thought.

Do you think the agent had really forgotten to get the caller's name? No way. The agent just wanted the caller to think so. It's psychology. Suppose the first thing the agent asked was the caller's name. Such a question can immediately place callers on the defensive. Consequently, they may hang up. The "what's your name?"

question was handled in such a manner as if agent and buyer were just chatting informally. Such a style can make buyers more at ease.

The agent didn't ask for the caller's telephone number right away. He wanted to avoid turning the "chat" into an interrogation. Instead, the agent set the stage to create a good mood and requested the name and telephone number only when he felt comfortable asking for them.

Right now, the caller is on hold. How long should the caller be left there? Just a few seconds, long enough for the agent to get the necessary information. When the agent returns, he can jump right back into the track by asking what it was about a particular ad that caught the caller's attention. This is the beginning of the process to determine whether the caller is a looker or a buyer. The best time to do this is at the beginning of the call, and it can be done by asking a variety of questions.

STOCK QUESTIONS

Questions designed to learn information about the caller are referred to as stock questions. An agent wouldn't begin a sales conversation by asking, "Gordon, are you ready to buy right now?" Gordon may be ready, and he may know it. But such directness could be misconstrued as a high-pressure tactic. The agent doesn't want to turn off a buyer.

Be easy. There's plenty of time.

An easy question is, "Gordon, what was it about that ad that caught your attention?" That's a nice soft question that can be asked, just out of curiosity. But the answer can give plenty of insight into the caller's situation.

In this case, Gordon said he favors untraditional homes. In another case, a caller may indicate a preference for two-story homes or a particular area of town. Whatever the caller says, it should be written down. In a few minutes, the agent will do something with the answers.

The next question is, "How long have you been looking for a home?" That's a fair question. The answer can help an agent determine whether the caller is a looker or a buyer. In this case, Gordon had been looking for about two months. If he had said seven months, the agent could deduce that Gordon is too fussy. If the answer was, "Since yesterday," then the agent could assume that Gordon needs some education in house hunting.

Then the agent asks Gordon, "Have you worked with any brokers at all?" Gordon had not. That tells the agent that Gordon has been calling from advertisements and has not been looking seriously. If he had said, "Sure, I know every broker in town," then the agent would know that he is a serious looker but, for one reason or another, has not been able to find the right house.

"Have you looked at many houses?" The answer would tell an agent whether the caller is in the habit of calling from advertisements.

"Of the houses you've seen, what was it about them that you didn't like?" The agent needs to become familiar with what the caller doesn't like in homes to know what type of properties to avoid. Again, all answers should be written down.

IDENTIFY THE PROBLEM

With all these answers, an agent can analyze and identify a caller's plight before the conversation is finished. If done properly, the caller will be motivated to come into the office, and that's exactly what the agent wants. Callers will visit agents for their own reasons more willingly than for agents' reasons.

So what do we have from Gordon? He's looking for an untraditional home, and he's been looking for about two months. If a buyer has been looking in vain for any kind of home for two months, it's probably because the buyer hasn't been working with a conscientious real estate agent.

We learned that Gordon hasn't been working with any other brokers. This should reveal that he is only calling from advertisements. Odds are Gordon is getting nowhere, because most of the time, people don't buy houses they see advertised in newspapers.

We know Gordon doesn't like the houses he has seen, because the rooms are too small. That means Gordon is looking at homes that he shouldn't be seeing.

So what is Gordon doing? He's wasting time.

A good agent could help him out by asking what he wants to know about the property. Nine times out of ten, the first question will be, "What's the address?"

Smart agents won't tell.

DON'T TELL THE ADDRESS

The agent told Gordon that studies indicate that most people don't buy the house they first see advertised. And rather than waste Gordon's time, the agent suggested more conversation about the property before revealing the address.

That seemed to suit Gordon just fine. Most of the time, the same explanation will suit your prospects, too. And, then, you can get right back on track.

Most callers won't ask for the address a second time. Of course, some ask not only a second time, but a third time. But this track offers an infallible system of not giving away addresses anymore.

Learn to set the question aside. Use "Moneymaker No. 1." (For example, "What's the address?" "No problem, but first, let me tell you that studies indicate that most buyers don't purchase the home they first saw. . . .")

The average agent either would have given out the address or would have tried to fight the caller by saying the seller requested the address not be released. But that's fighting too soon. Callers should be kept comfortable and away from their defensive natures.

Some callers will insist on fighting every step of the way. Ultimately, the agent will lose them because they will hang up. If that happens, nothing is really lost. If an agent is destined to lose a prospect, it's better to lose one early, rather than after counting on one for a sale.

The key is to realize that every caller is not a prospect. Remember what the Bible said about seeking the living among the dead. Most callers won't insist on fighting. The call detailed in this chapter is very typical. Gordon asked for the address, but the agent stayed on track. Gordon may not have been really comfortable answering questions, but he did anyway. The agent gathered valuable information which spelled out Gordon's problem. And the agent got the information by asking questions.

But an agent can't ask stock questions all day. The caller deserves a chance to ask questions, too.

Good agents give the caller a chance to get some answers. They don't subscribe to the theory that a question should be answered with a question. For example, "Does the house have a family room?" is an honest question. But for an agent to reply, "Do you want it to have one?" says absolutely nothing. That's all "take" and no "give." The agent gets information, but the caller gets none in return. Such an approach might prompt the caller to call another agent.

Good agents answer the caller's questions, but they don't lose control of the call. For each question they answer, they ask one in return.

"How many bedrooms does it have?" the caller asks. "It has three bedrooms," the agent replies. "Is that what you're looking for?" This puts the proverbial ball right back into the caller's court.

After answering the agent's question, the caller will ask another. The agent should answer, then ask another. It's like ping-pong.

When the caller asks about price, good agents don't beat around the bush. They reveal the price. It's practically public knowledge anyway. But good agents don't forget to maintain control. If they stop there, they will lose it.

After giving the price, the agent should ask a positive question, such as "Were you thinking of investing more?" That forces the caller to answer again.

The question shouldn't be negative. Most agents would say, "The house costs $94,500. Is that too much for you?" Keep the questions upbeat and positive.

IF IT'S OPINION, SAY SO

If the caller asks a question that calls for an opinion, the agent should clearly state that the answer is simply his or her point of view. In this case, Gordon asked if the house is located near a school. The agent thought so but said it depended on what Gordon considered to be close.

My father used to tell me that he, as a boy, would trudge five miles through snow to school. Whether or not he actually did, I suspect he would consider three miles or less to be within easy walking distance. But three miles for today's youth (even for those of my day) is a bit much. But good agents never second-guess the caller, who may think that four blocks amounts to driving distance.

The same principle applies with a "size" question, such as "What size is the living room?" What kind of an answer is "large." That could mean the size of a football field.

Good agents qualify their answers. They give specific answers, and they let callers draw their own conclusions to avoid misunderstandings. But they always tie-down the caller with a question, such as "Does eighteen by twenty-four feet sound large enough for you?"

The agent and the caller are trading information. Every time agents give an answer, they should ask a question designed to let them know what the buyer is thinking. The more practice, the smoother the performance.

So practice, drill and rehearse. Practice with another agent until you become comfortable with the track. The words aren't as important as the basic concept behind the track itself. Once you know each step of the track, your words will flow naturally.

GET THE BUYER'S ATTENTION

Now it's time to close for the appointment. First, the agent must command the buyer's attention. Selling to an inattentive prospect is a waste of time. Words simply go into one ear and out the other.

How do you get a buyer's attention over the telephone? Sometimes, you might feel like blowing a whistle into the mouthpiece or, better yet, firing a .45-caliber pistol two inches away. But that's really not good for human relations.

Instead, you'll command attention by identifying the buyer's problem and offering a solution. In this case, Gordon was looking for a unique home that may never reach the newspaper. If Gordon looks only through newspapers for a special house, he may never find it.

So invite the buyer to your office, where you can share information on all types of homes. If you don't have anything suitable, you can at least find out exactly what the buyer wants so you can find it before another agent does.

Suppose Gordon had been working with other brokers. Then he would have had another problem. Buyers who won't work exclusively with one agent may find that none of the agents will work diligently for them, since the odds are increased that each agent might not get the sale.

It's like going to three attorneys with a criminal case and telling each of them you'll only pay the attorney who wins the case. What kind of cooperation would you get? Little, if any.

Real estate agents are the same way. If a customer is working with three to five agents, none of them will devote the necessary effort toward finding the suitable home. Stress the benefits of exclusivity to a caller. An agent will work harder for a prospect if he or she knows there is no competition for the commission.

If Gordon had looked at a dozen or more homes, instead of just a couple, then an agent would know that Gordon hadn't been properly qualified and is wasting a lot of time and gas looking at the wrong houses. Remember, your job is to help prospects see that they have problems and that you can not only share with them alternate solutions, but you can also assist them in solving their problems. It's that simple.

IN A CAPSULE

1. When getting a call from an advertisement, find out if the caller is a looker or a buyer. Don't spend much time with lookers. They'll waste your time. Remember, seek not the living among the dead.

2. Develop the right "floor-time" attitude. Realize that each caller may have $1,000 that you can earn.

3. There are four components to good communication: the sender, the message, a method of conveying the information and a receiver. The agent is the sender and is responsible for conveying the right message, which is to entice prospects to come into the office to be qualified. It's a mistake to show a home until the prospect is qualified.

4. Use the "ad-caller" track when talking with a caller. Find out what particular "problem" the caller has by asking stock questions. Then, motivate the caller to come to your office by identifying the problem and offering to help find its solution.

5. Do not give out the address of the advertised home. You will do neither yourself nor the caller any favor. In most cases, callers don't buy homes they see advertised in the newspapers.

List the most important points you have gained from the
preceding Strategy:

_____

_____

_____

_____

_____

_____

_____

_____

_____

_____

_____

_____

_____

_____

_____

_____

8

Separate Lookers from Buyers

There's a funny thing about houses and cars. They're both necessities of life. Yet, they're both regarded as status symbols to the extent that people often estimate your net worth by the size and type of house in which you live and automobile which you drive.

Of course, not everyone can afford to live in mansions or drive expensive vehicles. But everyone can dream, and many people dream their dreams not only at home, but also at real estate offices and automobile dealerships. And that's where a lot of real estate agents run into trouble. They waste their time showing houses to people who can't afford them. (Car salespeople undoubtedly have the same problems, but that's not our concern).

This wasted time could have been spent showing those houses to prospects who could afford them. And if the agent had taken the time to qualify the buyer, he or she would have known whether the prospect was a bona fide buyer or a time-wasting looker.

Remember, seek not the living among the dead. When agents fail to qualify buyers, they waste their time showing houses to people who can't afford to do anything but dream. And dreams not only can't buy houses, but they also won't pay your bills.

Don't get me wrong, there's nothing wrong with dreaming. Some of the biggest, most inspiring success stories in the world started because somebody had a dream. But dreamers really should dream on their own time, not on someone else's.

So it's highly important that you learn to qualify buyers, so you can:

1. *Show them the houses they can afford.* To do anything else is a gross waste of time.

2. *Eliminate any future objections.* Buyers possibly might put off agents by saying they want to look around some more. They may have that urge because they weren't properly qualified. They may not know that they are eligible only for a certain range of potential properties.

3. *Eliminate fall-throughs.* Those are almost certain sales that don't work out. The seller accepts an offer, the agent begins the process of closing the sale and then, for one reason or another, the buyer isn't approved for a loan.

4. *Establish trust.* The agent confirms the buyer can afford houses in a particular price range, and the buyer depends upon the agent to find the best house for the money.

It's virtually always better to work with all cards faced up on the table. It's in the best interest of both the agent and the potential buyer.

KEYS TO QUALIFICATION

Separating lookers from buyers is a rather simple process. In fact, there are only two steps that must be taken to determine whether you have a looker or a buyer on your hands, and the first step is up to the buyer.

Step No. 1 in separating a looker from a buyer is CITO. Remember that? The agent wants the buyer to "Come Into The Office." If a buyer agrees to come into the office, then he or she is at least more serious about buying than the caller who isn't willing to come in. Or, to put it another way, a buyer who is willing to come to the office is half-way qualified.

Step No. 2 involves a simple rating system, closely akin to a rating system I offered in chapter two. Remember the plus-minus rating system for prospects on motivation to move and ability to move? You can use a similar system during the qualification. Make three categories, one for motivation, another for ability and the third for urgency. After asking your qualification questions, give the buyer either a plus or minus under each category.

For example, does the buyer merely desire to move, or must the buyer move? If the buyer only desires to move, give him or her a minus. But give a plus if the buyer must move. For ability, does the buyer have the necessary capital to buy? If so, give a plus. If not, give a minus. For urgency, does the buyer have to buy a new home within ninety days, or does he or she have a year or more during which to buy? If the buyer must buy within ninety days or less, give a plus. Otherwise, give a minus.

When you're finished, if you have three pluses, you have a buyer who is likely to purchase very soon. Anything less than three pluses may indicate that you have, for whatever reason, a non-serious buyer. For example, a buyer with adequate finances and motivation to relocate still may decide not to buy if there is no urgency. If the buyer is comfortable with his or her present home, he or she may eventually find a reason not to buy. On the other hand, a buyer whose house has just burned down would have the motivation to relocate quickly, but the buyer still may not be worth your time because he or she may also be bankrupt.

If you would make the most money you're capable of earning, you can do it only by spending your time with buyers who are most likely to buy. That means, quite frankly, that you must weed out the lookers and get rid of them. Don't work with anyone who isn't chomping at the bit, so to speak, to buy a new home and who doesn't have the necessary resources to purchase.

QUALIFY THE BUYER

After you've established a rapport with the buyer (that is, get the buyer to like and trust you, just like you would with a potential seller), you'll want to work toward the objective of this meeting— to qualify the buyer. Don't be too anxious. Don't ask, "How much money do you make?" Be easy. Gradually begin qualifying by, perhaps, offering a visual presentation designed to highlight the benefits of doing business with you and your company.

Sit down with the buyer, at your desk, or in a private conference room, and say, "Before we begin, let me first show you some of the services that our company offers to help buyers, like yourselves, find the right home at the right price in the shortest period of time."

Then you might take the following steps with buyers:

a. Fill out a qualification sheet to determine their wants, needs, likes, dislikes and motivations for buying.

b. Show them a copy of the multi-listings book (a collection of available listings), along with the multi-photo book that your company may keep for prospective buyers. Explain that you have access to all the properties.

c. Show them a list of satisfied customers (remember to ask for testimonials; they don't take much effort, but they make quite an impact on prospects).

d. Show them a copy of the offer to purchase and the agreement of sale, so you can reassure them that the forms are just standard and, until they are signed, remain as routine work-sheets. That's good salesmanship.

Now it's time to qualify them in terms of financial abilities and property needs and desires. For example, if they definitely will not consider a home without a basement, their selection is substantially reduced right away. Find out what is motivating them to move. Have they, as a family, grown out of their current home, or are they wanting to scale down to a smaller one? Are they moving because of increased or decreased income?

A word of caution on financial qualification: Don't overqualify. For example, an established physician looking for a $175,000 to $200,000 home shouldn't be asked about his or her income. The question won't sound professional.

Instead, ask basic financial questions pertaining to the purchase itself. Find out how much money the good doctor plans to invest in the new home.

Invest! Isn't that a good word? Don't ask how much money the doctor wants to pay each month. Ask instead how much of a monthly investment is being considered. Again, many times in this business, it's not what is said that counts so much as how it is said.

When it's time to ask questions about wants and needs, be thorough. Find out everything you need to know. At a minimum, how many bedrooms do the buyers want? At a minimum, what size of a lot do they need? Is a family room or a garage absolutely necessary?

Question potential buyers every step of the way. Fill out the buyer qualification form with them. Do they have any hobbies? Do they need an extra room? Are they interested in a large or small lot? Do they have any particular likes concerning area and location?

But don't carve the buyers' likes and dislikes into stone. They can change. Many times, potential buyers don't know what kind of a house they want—until they actually see it.

WIDEN THE SELECTION

Buyers can really be convinced they want a three-bedroom, brick home located in a particular neighborhood and costing no more than "X" amount of dollars, provided the home includes a finished basement and a garage. Yet, these same people may actually buy a two-bedroom condominium with no basement and only a carport that costs "X" plus $5,000.

People buy the first home for which they get a good feeling. They don't necessarily know in advance which home they're going to buy.

The more specific characteristics sought, the harder it will be to find a suitable home. Agents who over qualify actually limit their selections, and this is not good when it comes to earning commissions.

Agents instead should widen their selections. Suppose Mr. and Mrs. Buyer say they require four bedrooms. The average agent would write down "four bedrooms," just because the buyers said so. The average agent believes buyers should know what they want. But that's not necessarily so.

Good agents ask buyers if, for the right price, they would accept three bedrooms, or five. If they say they can, then the selection has been widened. If the buyers say they would like to live south of Main Street, don't stop there. Widen your selection. It's easy. Just ask, "If I found the right home at the right price, but it happened to be a little bit north of Main Street, would you even consider it? Or should we forget it?" If Mr. and Mrs. Buyer would ever buy a home north of Main Street, they will say that they will consider another area. That means you have just increased your odds of making a sale.

Perhaps your next question would be, "Do you need a basement?" And they say, "Oh, yes, we'd love to have one." Then you might say, "If the price is right and the first floor is large enough, would you consider a home without a basement?" If they say they will, then you've widened your selection again, further increasing the odds of making a sale.

Of course, it's very possible that the buyers will say, "Under no circumstances will we consider a home without a basement. We've got six children, and we must have some place in which to lock them every now and then." Then you can rest assured (for the most part) that they won't buy a home without a basement. (I still wouldn't bet my commission on it, though.)

Below are six questions specifically designed to help you widen your selection of homes for your prospects. Get into the habit of asking these questions regularly:

1. What's the maximum amount of cash you have to invest in a house?

2. For the right house, could you go any higher?

3. What's the maximum monthly investment you'd like to make?

4. For the right house, could you go any higher?

5. What is it that you want in a home in terms of extras, such as a fireplace, dishwasher, basement, attic, garbage disposal, etc.?

6. Which of these things could you do without if you had
    no choice?

LET BUYERS PARTICIPATE

When selecting properties to tour, it's important to let the buyers participate in the search. Suppose they don't. Instead, the agent might say, "Listen, have I got the perfect home for you! And just in case that one isn't, this other one I have in mind may be. Let's make arrangements to see both of them." The buyers may feel like they're being set up because they didn't participate in the search. Even if it turns out to be the home that they want and need, they still won't feel comfortable buying it because they'll feel they haven't seen the widest possible selection.

So take buyers through every step of the search. Show the multi-listings book to them and explain that it contains practically every listing available in the area. Then point out that every home in the book isn't for them. Show them that, based on their information, you can narrow down to several pages the number of possibilities that would suit their needs.

NARROW THEIR SELECTION

This literally narrows their selection, just after you've widened it. You're showing the buyers that they don't have a great selection anymore. This is psychologically sound. When the buyers tour the right home, you don't want them thinking that there are scores of others from which to choose.

I hope that makes sense to you. The last thing you need are indecisive buyers. If they think the town is filled with suitable houses, they may never buy, and that benefits neither them nor you.

Now that buyers have only three to four pages in the multi-listings book to consider, start the selection process. Keep possession of this book, but go over it with them one page at a time, so they can see that you are considering every house on each page.

Why look at the multi-listings book first, instead of your office listings? If you first try to sell them on your office listings, they may feel intimidated. They might think they're being set up, and you don't want the buyer to feel badly, or uncomfortable, about buying.

So, refer to the multi-listings book, then go to your office listings. Let the buyers select properties they might want to see. Make sure they are within the buyers' qualification range. Be sure the buyers like the basic features, such as number of bedrooms and basic location. When you do take them out to see the property, they will feel that this is their only selection, and they'll be more comfortable making a decision.

CALL THE SELLERS

Once the buyers have selected properties, the best thing you can do is excuse yourself for a few minutes and go to a private telephone, away from the buyers, so you can call the sellers.

Some sellers can be difficult. Sometimes, agents try to arrange appointments to show properties, and the seller talks to them as if they were debt collectors.

It's strange. The sellers say they want to sell, but they act as if they're inconvenienced when buyers come to tour. An agent could almost get the impression the sellers expect the house to be sold, sight unseen.

An agent might call the seller and say, "Listen, I've got this couple interested in looking at your home, and we would like to come over some time within the next hour. Would that be all right?"

It would seem the seller would be elated that the agent may have found a buyer for the home. But it doesn't always work out that way. "Don't come over now, the house is a mess," the seller might say. Or, "Not today, I'm getting ready to go shopping. Next time, give me a couple of hours notice."

The agent is trying his or her level best to get the house sold, and the sellers are fighting every step of the way. They are probably the same people who refused to post a yard sign because they don't want it widely known that their house is for sale.

Strange, isn't it? But if you stay in the business long enough, you'll know I'm telling you the truth. Remember that the seller's resistance to showing the property is your cue to come back with a concerned tone. For example, the dialogue might go something like this:

AGENT: Is your home still on the market?

SELLER: Of course.

AGENT: Do you want to sell it?

SELLER: Why, yes.

AGENT: Okay. We may have a problem. I've got some qualified buyers who need to buy a house soon, and I've got three houses lined up to show them today. I think yours might be the right house, but the buyers must see it first. And if they don't get to see it, they may decide to buy one of the other two. I sure would hate to see you miss out.

Then give the seller a little "ice cream." That is, you should calmly plead with and encourage the seller to let you do your job, which is, sell the house. But don't be harsh! That's why we say to give the sellers some "ice cream." Talk to the uncooperative seller like a daddy or mommy would encourage a child.

You might try, "Look, just this time could I please ask you to postpone your shopping, or would you please leave a key with a neighbor? If you want, we'll look at your house first, so you can go ahead with your day."

If the seller refuses, you may wonder why they even bothered to put their house on the market at all. But most of the time, if you pleasantly but firmly insist, the sellers will give in. That's when you should thank them profusely, to make them feel good about letting you sell their house for them. Then tell them that you and the couple will arrive there within a general period of time, such as during the next hour.

Don't commit yourself to a specific time. If you say that you will be there at 3 P.M., you'll likely meet with a cool reception should you arrive at 3:10. Don't set yourself up for a conflict. You don't want to offend the seller. If all goes well with the tour, you could be negotiating with the seller within a couple of hours.

So if sellers give you a reason why you shouldn't visit, put your persuasion skills to work. Tell them how beneficial it can be to reconsider. It could make all the difference in whether or not they will be able to move on schedule.

IN A CAPSULE

1. Qualify buyers. It's important. It's the first step to show them houses they can afford, eliminate future objections, avoid fall-throughs and establish trust.

2. When qualifying the buyer, carefully ask qualifying questions. Use the word "invest" instead of "spend." Have the buyer fill out qualification forms. Detail what services your company offers and how you will be able to serve them.

3. Widen buyers' selections by asking them if they would accept more or less in a home for the right price and location. This will help you in your selection process. And it will help the buyers, because buyers tend to purchase the first home for which they get a good feeling.

4. Let the buyers participate in the search. If they don't tour enough homes, they may feel they didn't have a good selection from which to choose. Review available listings with your buyers to make them certain you've conducted a thorough search.

5. Narrow the selection. After you've widened it, then narrow it down by showing them that other homes may cost more or lack many features that the original selection contains.

6. When you find a selection for your buyer, make sure the seller will agree to show it. If the seller hesitates, stress that the sale may be lost. Insist on the showing by offering to come right away, or at the earliest convenient time.

List the most important points you have gained from the
preceding Strategy:

_____

_____

_____

_____

_____

_____

_____

_____

_____

_____

_____

_____

_____

_____

_____

_____

9

Demonstrating Properties

I'm opening this chapter by giving you a tip that may go against what you've already been taught. In fact, I've been told time and time again that this is one of the most unusual pieces of advice that I offer. But it has its benefits, which I will detail.

But first, the advice: Once you've cleared the way for the showing of the house, take only the prospective buyers with you. Take nothing else—no visuals, no information, no charts and, by all means, no multi-listing books.

And if there happens to be a multi-listing book in your car when you and the buyers begin the trip to the house, I would advise you to sit on it!

It's happened more than once that an agent shows a house to a buyer, who likes it and is thinking about buying. Then, he or she spots the multi-listing book in the car and says: "Look, Dear, here are hundreds of houses from which to choose. There's no hurry."

There are two reasons to go on this trip empty-handed. First, you want to get the buyers back to the office, which puts you in the best position to sell a house. Also, extra material isn't necessary, because the best salesmanship in the world can't sell a house to buyers who aren't interested. If your buyers don't want the house, a tractor-trailer load of extra material, photographs, testimonials and business flyers won't change their minds.

What if they do want the house? You still don't need the material. The buyers will be happy (most of the time) to return to the office with you to learn more about the house.

Of course, don't argue with people who demand to buy. If they make it clear they want to purchase immediately, sign the purchase agreement on the fender of your car. But ordinarily, the office is the place to be, and prospective buyers will go there for their own reasons faster than they'll go for yours.

When selecting properties for your buyers to tour, don't try to set them up. Select at least three homes, each with a good chance of being the home that will appeal strongly to the buyer.

Suppose you show a prospective buyer two lousy homes and one "cream puff." The buyers are going to realize they're being set up. Not only can this tactic ruin your credibility, but it also fights the odds. Buyers who see only one appealing home are not likely to buy. They haven't seen enough houses to know if they've found what they want. Agents have a better chance of making a sale by making three strong selections.

Perhaps you'll want to save your own listing to sell to your buyers. That's entirely up to you. But make sure all the properties you select are viable possibilities for the buyers.

Now you and the buyers are ready to leave the office to tour one of the selected properties. Whose car do you take? Yours. Always. For three good reasons:

1. If you drive, it leaves their eyes free to see the area.

2. You have control of the situation.

3. With you behind the wheel, you increase the odds of getting the buyers back to the office.

I hope you know what to talk about while driving. In fact, there's only one thing you absolutely should not discuss—real estate. Talk about anything else that will interest your buyers, but leave real estate alone for the moment. There will be plenty of time to discuss real estate later. Give the buyers a break.

SET THE STAGE

Just before arriving at the house, prepare the buyer for the tour. Don't talk about what a great house you're going to show. Don't tell the buyers how much they will enjoy it.

On the contrary. Prepare the buyer for the worst. Do not rave about how clean and neat the house is, or how it must have been built with them in mind. You'll actually benefit by making the buyers think that the house may be a little disappointing. If you build the buyers' expectations by telling them they are about to tour a truly fine home, you'll be setting them up for quite a fall should they not like it. In fact, you'll actually increase the odds of them not liking it, because they'll be looking for drawbacks. If they do like it, they won't really be surprised, because you prepared them for it.

But if you say, "I believe this is the house that could stand some cleaning. I'll let you be the judge of that," then you're letting them know not to get very excited. They'll be prepared for disappointment. And that's the best way to set up someone for a pleasant surprise.

171

There's also a practical reason for this advice. As a teenager, I had a friend named Jasper Scaglioni. All the guys used to go to his house and eat twelve-course dinners. Mrs. Scaglioni, a good Italian woman, was quite a cook. She fed the whole neighborhood at one time or another.

And let me tell you, Mrs. Scaglioni prided herself on her meals and her home. If she wasn't cooking, she was cleaning. That good woman spent her life keeping up her home by cooking and cleaning, cleaning and cooking. . . .

My point is, if you take Mrs. Scaglioni on a tour of a house and tell her in advance that the house is clean . . . it had better be clean! And if it turns out that it isn't, she will indeed let you know— in no uncertain terms.

What's clean to you may not be clean to a person like Mrs. Scaglioni. And that's my point. Describing something as "clean" is a value judgment. What you consider clean may be a pig pen to someone like Mrs. Scaglioni.

So you'd be better off to say, "I think this is the house that could use some elbow grease. If I remember correctly, it needs a little sprucing up."

The worst that can happen is the prospective buyer will say, "You're right. This place is a dump. Let's go." Then again, the buyer might say, "Hey, this isn't so bad. I can't believe you thought this was dirty. I'll buy it."

This reminds me of my very first listing in the real estate business many years ago in Warren, Michigan. My trainer went with me, because it was one of my first leads. When we arrived, I went into shock. The house actually leaned to one side, and it was in such a state of disrepair, I was amazed it hadn't been condemned.

So much for the exterior. Once inside, we discovered that six German shepherds also lived there. They could enter and leave at will through an exit trap in the rear door designed especially for dogs. To say the house smelled of dog would be kind. There was an odor so intense that . . . well, let's not go into that. Just take my word for it, the place smelled!

I got my first listing (it wasn't difficult). But I wasn't necessarily proud of it. On the way back to the office, I remember saying to my trainer, "Hey, do we have to tell anybody about this one?" I thought there was no way in the world the home would ever sell.

About three weeks later, I was at my desk and my trainer said, "Hey, Floyd, I want you to show Sidonie (the name of the street on which the house was located). I thought, "You rat! Making me show that house. . . ."

All the way over to the house, I apologized to the prospective buyers for the condition of the home, trying to prepare them for the worst. I must have done a good job. The couple walked through the front door. Instead of screaming, the woman said, "Oh, this is kind of cute."

I just stood there with my mouth open.

A few hours later, I sold the home. It was my first double-dip on my very first listing. And in the process, I learned a lesson that's true universally.

You never know what a prospect will think of a home. So don't oversell. If you must say anything about the house to prospective buyers, criticize it. If, instead, you describe it as a real "cream puff," you're likely to talk your way out of a sale.

If it's an excellent house, say it's good. If it's good say it's fair. If it's fair, say it's poor. And if it's poor, tell them they will get more home for their money. This will increase your odds of pleasantly "surprising" them.

GET RID OF THE SELLER

Has a seller ever gotten in your way while showing a home? Perhaps the seller took an active role in showing the house and making comments to the buyer. Every time you tried to take control, the seller interrupted and eventually took over the showing. When sellers do this, they often talk the buyers out of buying.

Keep the seller out of the way. I've learned the hard way that just asking them to steer clear doesn't work. Asking them to leave the key for you won't solve the problem, either. They sometimes insist on staying there so they can help show the house.

I've learned over the years to give the seller a bit of "ice cream." I'd say, "Mr. and Mrs. Seller, we'll be over within the hour, but the buyers seem to be the type of people who like to discover things on their own. So could you, for a while, sort of pretend you're busy while we're over there?"

This works. I don't know why, but there's something about the word "pretend." I think everyone is just an overgrown child, at times. It's psychology. The sellers will think they are part of an elaborate plot to sell their homes. I've heard men pound away at workbenches they haven't touched in six months because I asked them to pretend they were busy.

When you arrive at the residence with the potential buyers, ask them to wait for you in the car. When the seller comes to the door, offer your card, tell why you're there and repeat, "By the way, we can increase the odds of selling the house if you pretend you're busy, because the buyers seem to be the type who like to discover things all by themselves."

ACT NONCHALANT

What kind of an attitude should you have while showing the property? I would describe it as "controlled nonchalance." I don't know if there is such a thing, but that's how I'd identify it.

If you oversell a home, a buyer is going to feel intimidated to buy. I recommend an attitude of casual nonchalance, but always be in control. When you walk in the front door with the buyer, you might say something like, "Well, you know what you're looking for, so why don't you walk around and I'll follow. By the way, if I find something I think you should see, I'll just point it out. Fair enough?"

Let them walk around. Don't necessarily lead the way, but control the situation. Don't let them miss anything that might interest them. For example, if they miss a very important linen closet, be sure they don't overlook it.

There are two major things you want to do while demonstrating properties. First, ask many questions. Second, get the prospect to participate in the demonstration. For example, does it hurt to say to the buyer, "Here is a door. Why don't you open it and see what's inside?"

What's the point? You probably already know what's behind it. But letting the prospect open it amounts to showmanship and participation. This increases your odds of selling the home. Have them check out the appliances of the kitchen, or to sit in the patio furniture to get a feel for the home.

But there's also a time for you to ask questions. And what kind of questions would you ask? Remember the "wopen" questions? They're good here, too.

You might ask them, "What do you think of the house?" or "What do you think of this room?" Get their impressions and their thoughts. Make statements of your own. But don't forget to tie down the statements with questions. "This is a large bedroom, isn't it?" "I'll bet you could have a huge housewarming party down here in this recreation room, couldn't you?" "Nice view, isn't it?"

IGNORE FIRST OBJECTIONS

Buyers will raise objections from time to time, but it doesn't mean that they won't buy the house. In fact, if you have ever bought a home, you'll agree when I say there's something about that home you don't like. Perhaps one of the rooms is too small, or the front lawn isn't spacious enough. The house might be too close to the property line, or not close enough to the driveway.

Prospective buyers are likely to buy a home even though there is something they don't like about it. Few, if any, homes are perfect. So when you're showing a house and the buyer hits you with an objection, ignore it. Suppose the buyer says, "Hey, Agent, the floor squeaks." Ignore it. Don't try to oversell it; don't try to explain it away. Don't even question it. Just ignore it.

The buyer might be thinking, "Gee, I sort of like this home. Maybe I should start looking for things I don't like." Or the buyer might be making a simple comment with no objection in mind. The less you say, the better.

If the buyer raises the objection a second time, you may have to do something about it. But try to ignore it the first time.

I've always thought women were better than men at selling real estate. Suppose a male agent is showing a couple around a home, and there is a heavy crack in the wall. The buyer asks if it can be fixed, and the agent says, "Sure," then launches into a detailed explanation of how it can be repaired. Meanwhile, the buyer is acting as if, "Well, maybe this house will be more trouble than it's worth."

But suppose a female agent is taking the same couple around the same house, and the couple noticed the crack in the wall. The female agent might ask, "Can it be fixed?" and the male buyer, motivated by his ego, would say, "Sure," then launch into a detailed explanation of how it could be repaired. In so doing, he might talk himself into buying.

ISOLATE THE OBJECTION

Sometimes, there is a major objection. Suppose the buyer points out that the driveway resembles a miniature rock quarry. Ignore it.

If the buyer points it out again, then you've got a good idea that the driveway bothers him.

Isolate the objection by saying, "Okay, the driveway needs a lot of work; but you do like the rest of the home, don't you?" This is called a trial close question. "Other than the driveway, is there anything else that bothers you about the home?"

If you hear the objection a second time, go ahead and attempt to close. If nothing else, maybe the buyer won't object again.

TURN NEGATIVES INTO POSITIVES

Work on the buyer's attitude by turning negatives into positives. Point out the drawbacks to the house in a positive manner. For example, if the bedrooms are small, you can say, "The architect designed this house to be economical. As you can see, he took the extra space off the bedrooms and added it to the living room and family room.

You could just be quiet about it and hope the buyer won't notice the small bedrooms; but that's not very likely, is it? Or you could just hope that the buyer won't notice that the house is built just to the south of some riding stables, to the east of a liquor distillery and to the west of a slaughterhouse, but that's not likely, either.

So what you say is, "Hey, I can get you a bigger house with bigger bedrooms, but it will cost you more." Or, "I can get you a house in a different location, but it will cost you more." "With this house, you'll get more home for the money. And you should act fast, because this is the only home we have where you can always tell from which direction the wind is blowing."

That might be a little tongue-in-cheek, but you get the picture. You can't afford to have a negative attitude if you're selling real estate. So don't allow negative aspects to cloud your mind. When negatives arise, turn them into positives.

TAKE NOTES

There is one thing you may take on a listing appointment—notes. Carry along a clipboard and paper, on which you may write down comments about the buyers' likes and dislikes of a particular home. Also, you can record some of the questions they have while you're demonstrating the property.

Don't take along a copy of the listing with you. There's a good reason for that. You don't want to answer all the questions they have while you're at the house. Get them back to the office.

Suppose a buyer asks, "Are the drapes included?" Even if you don't know, always respond with an answer and a controlled question, such as, "I'm not sure. Would you want me to see if I can get you these drapes?" Then write down the question. Or the buyer might say, "Does the seller plan to fix this ceiling?" And you answer, "Well, it's not mentioned in the listing; would you want me to see if the seller will fix the ceiling for you?" Then write down the question.

Now why should we ask trial questions? Because they provide ways to find out if the buyers are psychologically talking themselves into owning the house. Ask a lot of questions. This helps you understand how the buyers think. Do everything you can to find out whether this is the house for them. If it isn't, you won't sell it to them.

WATCH FOR BUYING SIGNALS

When do you close on a buyer? Whenever they start showing you buying signals. Those are things that the buyers do or say to indicate to the agent that they are placing themselves, at least in their minds, inside of the house.

For example, Mr. Buyer might be in the basement by the workbench, playing with the vise grip, or he may be opening doors and pacing around the rooms. A buying signal also may be a simple question, such as, "Do you think the seller would fix the ceiling?" That's a buying signal, because if he didn't like the house, the buyer couldn't care less about the ceiling. Another buying-signal question may be, "When is the seller going to move?" That's a tip-off that the buyer is interested. Again, if the buyer didn't care about the house, why would he care about the seller?

Sometimes, buying signals can be positive, like, "Oh, Dear, wouldn't our blue sofa look lovely in the living room?" Or, "Look, Honey, our bedroom furniture would look so nice in here, and what a nice view from the window."

And sometimes, buying signals can take seemingly negative forms. They might come from the male buyer who says, "Boy, it will take me three weeks to get this house into livable shape." This could be interpreted as criticism of the house, but since he's talking about doing the repairs himself, it would be better to view that statement as a positive sign.

So when you hear a buying signal, should you attempt to close for the sale? Not yet. You don't want to appear as if you're trying to force the sale. Be easy.

And on the second buying signal, close.

CLOSE SOFTLY

After you've shown the home, ask the prospects if they want to buy. The question, "Do you want to buy this home?" is too intimidating at this time. How can they answer that question when they don't have all the facts? But they don't know anything about the taxes and a host of other things.

Don't ask them to buy it. Instead, let me give you the softest—yet heaviest—closing question: "You kind of like this one, don't you?" That's a powerful question. Don't pin them down with direct questions. Ease them into the buying spirit.

OBLIGATION TO SELLER

What if they say they don't like it? Then ask, "Would you buy the home at any price?"

That question takes a lot of nerve. After all, how can you expect the buyers to purchase a house they don't even like? But you should ask the question anyway, because you have an obligation to the seller. When you gave the seller a copy of the listing, you pledged to do everything in your power to sell it. The least you can do for the seller when you show the home is to ask the buyers—even if they have already said they don't like the house—whether they would buy it at any price.

This question doesn't suggest that the seller will accept a lower price. But you may be surprised to find that the buyer might show interest in the property at the suggestion of a lower price. Then you can start negotiating.

On the other hand, the buyers may say, "No, we wouldn't have this house as a gift." What do you do then? Show them another house.

Or better yet, "demonstrate" another house. Don't sell too hard, just demonstrate. And when you get enough buying signals, ask your heavy-soft trial closes, and then take them back to the office.

IN A CAPSULE

1. Unlike the listing appointment, when showing a home, take nothing with you. If buyers ask questions, invite them to go with you to the office after the demonstration. This is the best place for them to be in terms of your closing.

2. Set the stage by preparing the buyer for the worst. It's the best and safest way to set up the buyer for a pleasant surprise. If you prepare the buyer for the best, you're actually setting him or her up for quite a fall.

3. Before showing a home, ask the seller to "pretend" to be busy. This keeps the seller out of the way and, at the same time, from saying too much. You don't want a seller to blow the sale.

4. Conduct the demonstration with controlled nonchalance, but always stay in control. Let buyers look around for themselves, but offer to help them if they need it. Be sure the buyers don't miss any important features of the home.

5. Ignore first objections. If a buyer says a room is too small, ignore it. There is nothing you can do about it, and trying to explain it might cost you a sale.

6. If the buyer raises the objections a second time, attempt to close by isolating the objection. No home is perfect. The buyer may want it anyway.

7. Turn negatives into positives. If there are any negative features in a home, prepare the buyer in advance by stressing positive features. For example, "The bedrooms in this house are small because the designer wanted to build a house economical on space. But you'll notice that the

space shaved off the bedrooms has been added on to the living room.'' Then tell the buyer you can get a house with bigger bedrooms, but it will cost more.

8. Take notes. Write down all of the buyers' questions. It's often helpful when closing or negotiating with the seller.

9. Watch for buying signals. Anything that indicates the buyer is putting himself or herself into the house on a permanent basis is a buying signal. For example, "Our bedroom suit would look good in here," or "This driveway is in such a state of disrepair, it will take me three weeks to get it smoothed out."

10. Close softly. Don't ask prospects if they'd like to buy. Ask instead something like, "You kind of like this one, don't you?" Don't intimidate the buyer.

11. Remember, you have an obligation to the seller to close. If the buyer doesn't act interested in the home, ask if the buyer would buy it at any price. You may get a positive response and a starting point for negotiation.

List the most important points you have gained from the
preceding Strategy:

_____

_____

_____

_____

_____

_____

_____

_____

_____

_____

_____

_____

_____

_____

_____

_____

_____

_____

10

Handling Stalls and Objections

Many years ago, there was a young man who felt he was not as successful as he should have been. He wasn't satisfied with his station in life. So he decided to sell his property and seek his fame and fortune elsewhere.

The man traveled around the world, all with one goal in mind— securing fame and fortune. Unfortunately, he got neither. And it was only on his deathbed as a poverty-stricken old man that he learned that the land he had sold off many years earlier had become one of the richest diamond mines in the world.

The title of this famous story is "Acres of Diamonds." I think there is a parallel between this story and the real estate business. There are too many agents who are not satisfied with their levels of production. Too often, they leave the business to seek their fame and fortunes elsewhere. Or they might stay in the business, yet hop from company to company, business to business.

Unlike the old man, the smart agents learn early that they can earn their "acre of diamonds" anywhere, provided they are willing to do what is necessary.

IT'S SIMPLE

Making money in the real estate business is simple. Theoretically and ideally, an agent has but to pick up a telephone and prospect, go on a listing appointment, break the ice, ask questions, talk pricing and get the listing.

Theoretically and ideally, the same process is involved with the buyers. The agent uses an "ad track," gets the buyers into the office, warms them up, qualifies them, selects properties and demonstrates them. The buyers select one, the agent fills out the purchase agreement, the buyers sign it, and that's it.

It's simple, isn't it? Yes, but it's not easy.

THE REAL WORLD

From the initial contact with buyers and sellers, agents are overloaded with obstacles. These obstacles might take the form of stalls, such as, "Not now, I want to think it over," or "I have a friend in the business, I don't need an agent." Or they might take the form of objections, such as "Thanks for calling, but I don't want to pay a commission," or "No, we don't want to buy this house."

Sometimes, when you do everything right in your listing and selling process, the prospects still won't sign. Instead, they hand you stalls and objections. If you're serious about real estate as a career, you'd better learn how to handle them. Then be prepared to close, close and close again.

Some time ago, some extremely reputable trainers and I were discussing the most important trait of a salesperson. Some of these trainers were very well known. They talked about the importance of a positive attitude, knowing how to prospect and good time management skills.

All of these things are important. But, I said, if you can't close, you can't sell. If you can't close, you're going to learn eventually that selling is not for you.

LEARN HOW TO CLOSE

Everything in the real estate business depends upon knowing how to close. When you call a "for sale by owner," does the seller say, "Oh, I'm so glad you called. Come on over right away for the listing?" No. You had to close, close and close again just to get the appointment. Still, you were guaranteed nothing. You had to close, close and close again just to get the listing. And you still have nothing unless the house is sold.

When a potential buyer called about an advertised home, you had to close, close and close again just to get the buyer into the office for qualification. Then you had to select several homes and close, close and close again when the buyer found one that really was appealing.

Once the buyer was convinced, you had to close, close and close again to get the seller to accept the offer. And if the seller instead made a counter offer, you had to close, close and close again to get the buyer to consider it.

Yet, agents say, "I want to sell real estate, but I don't want to close." But you can't sell real estate without closing.

Everything we do involves closing. Has a seller ever told you to put away your visual presentation and go ahead and produce the listing agreement? Have buyers ever called to say they wanted to come to your office for qualification and demonstration of three carefully selected homes? Has a seller ever automatically agreed to a price reduction without a word of protest? Most of the time, they fought every step of the way. You could have given up and, as a result, let some other real estate agent get the commission. But instead, you chose to fight back—without getting rough, of course.

And that's what closing is—not accepting a "no," but being pleasant about it. It's making a customer feel comfortable about something that, at least for the moment, he or she is not at all comfortable with.

To put it simply, closing is what selling real estate is all about. The success of any people business (and that's what the real estate business is) depends on salespeople motivating customers to make decisions with which they are not comfortable. This doesn't mean that agents are hustlers. No one can sell a house to a buyer who doesn't want it. It just can't be done.

Agents may attend seminars from now until doomsday. But until they learn to close, and sometimes close and close again, all those seminars are going to be for nothing. So since my discussion with the sales trainers, I have assembled a three-day, "blood, sweat and tears" closing bootcamp. More than two thousand real estate salespeople have attended, and we did nothing but learn to close, close and close again. We didn't talk about listing, financing or managing. All I taught them was how to muster the fortitude and use the techniques it takes to sell. Consequently, attendees were able to increase their business measurably, no matter how the real estate market was faring at the time.

So I'd like to share with you some highlights from my closing workshop. These are the most important things that we cover in that workshop to turn agents in a different direction—to help them overcome any fear or hesitation to close, close and close again.

YOU HAVE TO WORK

Selling real estate is like a buffet. Everything you want is right there before you, but you have to go after it, one thing at a time. Yet, at this proverbial buffet, most agents are starving, simply because of their unwillingness and/or inability to close enough sales.

Statistically speaking, eighty percent of all real estate agents from coast to coast will share only twenty percent of all commissions this year. That means that eighty percent of all commissions will be shared by the remaining twenty percent of agents. Some people have nothing to show for their efforts in the real estate business. They have plenty of time invested, but nothing to show. Yet, some agents are finding their fame and fortunes. The difference between the two is, the latter group has learned how to close successfully and consistently.

CONDITION YOURSELF

If you're sick with something more than a common cold or sore throat, you may go to the doctor for a diagnosis. Once you learn what is wrong, you can take the steps to treat it, so you can be well again.

Not being able to close is practically an illness. It can make you starve. And there are two reasons that people are not as strong, competent and confident as they should be.

1. *Negative conditioning.* We all have two minds, according to the science of psychocybernetics. One is the conscious mind, the other is the subconscious. The con-

scious mind is what we use to make an active decision, such as going for a walk, preparing dinner or driving a car. The subconscious mind is the warehouse. Everything that we sense, taste, touch, smell, hear or see goes into our subconscious mind, and it stays there forever.

Suppose you're sitting face-to-face with a seller, and now it's time to close. Your conscious mind sends a message to your subconscious. "Send me up a technique for closing, along with a side order of intestinal fortitude."

If the techniques are in your subconscious, you will get what you need. It's sent there by your sensormechanism, which is the link between the two minds. But the information must be there. If it isn't, you'll get nothing. And the only way to get the information in your subconscious warehouse is to practice, drill and rehearse.

2. **Inability to cut through stalls.** When a buyer puts you off, that's a stall. If you can't cut through it, you lose whatever it is that you want, be it a listing or a sale.

The difference between a stall and an objection is the difference between truth and fabrication. When a seller is reluctant to list with you, or a buyer is reluctant to buy, they have their reasons, as valid or invalid as they are. These are called objections.

But they won't always tell you the truth right away. For whatever reason, they don't want to tell you the real reason they are hesitant to buy or list. Instead, they hand you a reason for their inaction that differs from the truth. That's a stall.

You can't handle the objection without cutting through the stall. And until you cut through the stall, you won't get anywhere with your prospect. You've got to learn to understand stalls and objections, and how to handle both.

IT ISN'T EASY

The process of cutting through stalls and handling objections is not scientific. That means there are no sure-fire methods to produce results. People are complex and different. Most techniques for handling stalls and objections simply don't work most of the time. But all of the techniques work some of the time. You just don't know when certain ones will work.

So you'd better learn a lot of techniques, because you're going to need them in order to sell real estate.

OH, WELL, THAT DIDN'T WORK

Suppose you arrive at the seller's home, ring the doorbell, smile, pay a compliment, sit down at the kitchen table, make small talk, discuss the potential listing, tour the house, return to the table and ask for the listing. And the seller gives you a stall.

When prospects give you a stall, they're actually hiding. They don't want to make an immediate decision. And the best and most commonly used stall in the real estate business is, "I want to think it over."

No matter what you really think of the prospect's reason, pretend that you understand it. Agree with it.

"I can certainly appreciate how you feel about wanting to think it over," you might say. "And I definitely wouldn't want you to do anything with which you're not comfortable. But just out of curiosity, exactly what is it you want to think over? Is it price? Are you not sure I can sell your home? Are you a bit nervous about signing something?"

If the prospect levels with you, then you've got something to work with. More than likely, though, the prospect will say, "No, it's none of those reasons. I just want to think it over."

The average agent might think, "Ah, gee. That didn't work. Why did Floyd teach that technique if it isn't going to work?"

I'm warning you, they don't always work. These techniques are worse than the worst goof-offs at your office. They only work some of the time.

If you learn only one technique for handling stalls and objections, you might as well grab your unsigned listing agreement or offer to buy and head for the car. Instead, you must take the attitude, "Oh, well, that didn't work." Save the technique for another day, and try something else.

REASONS FOR OBJECTIONS

Objections usually fall into three categories. They either involve money, a lack of confidence in the agent or fear of the transaction itself.

1. *Money*. Perhaps a buyer thinks the monthly payment is too high, or the seller won't accept the buyer's offer because it's too low. On a listing appointment, the seller might claim the other broker said the house could bring more money. Or the seller may not want to list because he or she would rather sell the house without an agent and save the commission.

2. *Lack of confidence*. Remember L-I-S-T (lead-in, investigate, show and sell and tie-down)? If you didn't follow the process in its proper sequence, your prospects will

have a good reason for not being "sold," which can mean any one of a lot of things. A buyer may not be happy with your selections or may feel that you haven't demonstrated enough properties for a confident buying decision. Perhaps the buyer doesn't think he or she is getting the best home for the money.

Perhaps the seller isn't "sold" on you. As harsh as it seems, maybe the seller doesn't like you. Are personality clashes possible? Bet your commission on it. It could be the way you dress. Perhaps the seller doesn't see you as a successful real estate agent. For whatever reason, if the seller doesn't like you, you won't get the listing.

Of course, the chances are slim that a seller will actually say, "No, the reason I don't want to sign this listing tonight is I'm not sold on you." It would be much easier for the seller to hand you a stall, such as, "I'd like to think it over, and I'll get back with you."

3. *Fear.* Perhaps the buyer stalls because he or she is apprehensive about buying. The buyer may be thinking, "Wow, it's been years since I've bought a home. Why, when I bought my last home, interest rates were five percent. Now look at them! And I've read so much negative stuff in the newspaper lately about business and the economy. What if I sign this contract and something goes wrong and I can't get back my deposit?"

Suppose a potential seller who has owned a particular home for years is thinking about listing it. Perhaps the seller isn't sure that everything will work out satisfactorily. The seller may be afraid to list. It could just be negative conditioning on the seller's part. But you'll have to break through that barrier if the commission appeals to you.

When you get a stall, find the real objection (and that's no easy job!) and deal with it. Try to ease the prospect's doubts, then close. If the prospect offers another stall, break it down to the true objection, deal with it, and close.

And close, And close, And close.

CONDITIONS CAN'T BE HELPED

There is another aspect of the real estate business called a condition. That's the true reason why a transaction cannot occur.

For example, suppose you call a "for sale by owner." You reach Mr. Seller. You try to make a listing appointment, but Mrs. Seller is not at home. She left for work earlier, but not before having a serious discussion with Mr. Seller that might have gone something like this:

> "Sweetheart, let's have a serious talk. Let me tell you something. Today, our "for sale" ad started running in the newspaper, so that means you're going to hear from a lot of real estate agents. So I'm going to tell you in no uncertain terms: Don't invite any real estate agents over—not even to look at the house, not even to talk with us—for any reason. If a real estate agent calls, say that we're not interested, then hang up the phone. Do not talk to a real estate agent. Do not invite one over. I don't want to come home tonight and hear you've made even a tentative appointment. I'm not kidding you. Don't invite any real estate agents over here. I'm telling you, don't do it."

Back on the phone. You ask Mr. Seller for an appointment, and he tells you that he is not able to make one. The average agent would stop there. You shouldn't.

Try to schedule a tentative appointment, subject to his wife's approval, which in this case sounds unlikely. But you never know. Conditions are not permanent; they can change. Perhaps Mrs. Seller will get a promotion and a raise today, which could ease her resistance to talking with real estate agents. The worst that could happen is Mr. Seller would say, "I called my wife, and she told me to tell you that you'll be eaten by a Doberman if you come."

If that happens, don't go. Conditions can change, but you can't change them. A prospect who says, "I can't buy this, the payments are too high," may be stalling. If the prospect has been properly qualified, you should know.

On the other hand, the statement could be a condition. The buyer may not be able to afford the house. In that case, you just have to show the buyer less expensive homes.

That's why qualification is important. If you stay on track with people during the initial phases of L-I-S-T (lead-in, investigate, show and sell and tie-down), you can handle or eliminate in advance many of the objections and stalls you get.

WHEN TO HANDLE STALLS AND OBJECTIONS

Basically, there are a number of times to handle stalls and objections:

1. *Never.* Sometimes, you shouldn't do anything. Suppose you're on a listing appointment. You've broken the ice and you've asked permission to ask questions. Then the seller says, "I'm not paying any seven or eight percent commission." The worst thing you could do at that point would be to try and handle that objection. Instead, use Moneymaker No. 1: "No problem." Then get right back on track.

Or suppose you're showing a home to a buyer who raises an objection. "Boy, what an icky looking room!" the buyer says. What do you say? Nothing. Remember, ignore first objections.

2. *Later.* Suppose a buyer said. "This driveway is a disaster. I would have to replace the whole thing. And that's the only thing holding me back from buying this home." Don't stand at the driveway and try to overcome that objection. Simply say, "Fine, I've got an idea. Let's go back to the office, sit down and have a cup of coffee, and we'll talk about it. Maybe there's something we can do about it." Then you can handle the objection at the office.

3. *As they occur.* Suppose you've gone on a listing appointment, taken all the right steps then asked for the listing. And the seller said, "Wait, we want to think this over." You can't say, "Well, go ahead and sign, and we'll talk about it in a minute." Some objections and stalls have to be handled right as they occur.

4. *Before they occur.* If you know you're going to get an objection or stall, handle it before it arises. Suppose your buyers are a young couple who want their parents to look at the home before they buy it. The best time to overcome that objection is before you tour the property. Either talk them out of it, or have them take their parents along on the showing. There's no point in making two trips.

LET'S MAKE IT SIMPLE

If this sounds too complicated to handle, take heart. It's time add the simplicity factor. Remember, I told you that there are as many different objections and stalls as there are people. It's true, but all of those objections and stalls can be handled in one single objection track. No matter the problem, you can learn to deal with it by using a five-step formula:

- Agree with the objection.

- Feed back the objection.

- Isolate the objection.

- "Show and sell" with visuals.

- Close.

AGREE WITH THE OBJECTION

Perhaps a prospect will claim to have a friend in the business who will get the listing. You can respond by saying—not necessarily quickly, but naturally—"I can understand how you feel." That's a statement of agreement. This actually helps drop defense mechanisms, because whenever an objection is sounded, a defense wall automatically goes up. The agreement statement is designed to help drop the wall. It's psychologically sound.

You don't always have to say, "I appreciate how you feel." After a half dozen objections, you will sound like a broken record. There are other ways to say the same thing—"I can understand what you're saying," "Sure, that's no problem," "Well, I can certainly respect your opinion," "Well, I can empathize with that." Any way you want to say it, it means the same thing. But the main thing you should do is practice, drill and rehearse. Until you do that, you won't be comfortable with this track.

Here's another tip. In writing, you should avoid using ten words if you can say the same thing with only five words. But in selling, the opposite is true. Selling is not the time to be stingy with words.

Compare for yourself, "I appreciate how you feel," as opposed to, "Well, I can certainly appreciate how you must feel about that." You can create more of a feeling of agreement by using long statements.

And there is also voice inflection, which is important. It's not so much what you say as when and how you say it. Let's take for example the following sentence: I didn't say he kissed his wife. Let's see just how many different ways we might say it, without changing a word of the sentence. Instead, we'll only alter the emphasis placed on each word.

I didn't say he kissed his wife.

I *didn't* say he kissed his wife.

I didn't *say* he kissed his wife.

I didn't say *he* kissed his wife.

I didn't say he *kissed* his wife.

I didn't say he kissed *his* wife.

I didn't say he kissed his *wife*.

Voice inflection can give you control of the conversation. It can add believability to your words and it can be used to emphasize certain points. So agree with the objection, using voice inflection properly so you won't sound as if you're reciting a memorized line.

FEED BACK THEIR OBJECTION

This is a powerful tool. And how you feed it back depends on you, the buyer, the situation and what you've said before. Suppose someone said, "I have a friend in the business, and I may want to check with him/her before I sign this listing."

First, agree. "I can understand what you're saying." Then, feed back. "If I understand you right, what you mean is you're just going to talk first with your friend, then you'll feel more comfortable about signing this listing. Is that right?" This technique allows prospects to hear the objection in such a manner that it gives them something to think about.

Sometimes, repeating the objection might take the simplest form. That is, the objection is repeated as it was sounded. If someone told you, "I don't want to pay a commission," then repeating it in its simplest form would be verbatim—"If I understand you right, you don't want to pay a commission. Is that right?"

What do you get out of repeating it? You get the prospects thinking about their objection by feeding it back to them. And this also gives you time to think about your next move. But more importantly, once you get into the habit of agreeing and feeding back, you can use the concept as a powerful sales tool.

Let's say you are talking with a young couple considering buying a home. You've established quite a rapport. Everyone is getting along. Then they say they would like to delay signing the purchase agreement until they can get their parents to look at the home.

Agree and feed back. "No problem. That's your decision. But correct me if I'm wrong. You mean to say you want your parents to okay the home that you're going to buy?"

Be sure the feedback statement always ends in a question, such as "Is that right?", or "Is that what you mean?", or "Am I correct in assuming this?"

Remember, practice, drill and rehearse.

ISOLATE THE OBJECTION

This step is as powerful as the feedback statement. It forces prospects to admit if the objection is their only one. And equally as important, it gets prospects to commit to a decision.

A prospect doesn't want to pay a commission. The agent says, "I can appreciate how you might feel about not wanting to spend money. You are just dead set against paying anybody to sell your house, is that correct?"

To isolate the objection, the agent might ask, "If I could prove that you could get more money by letting me sell your home, would you list with me tonight?"

The isolation statement and the tie-down question force a prospect to commit to a decision or admit there are other objections. Of course, the agent must prove the claim, but the isolation statement determines if the stated objection is the only factor blocking the transaction.

Suppose a prospect says, "Maybe I should look at a couple of other houses before I actually decide." What should the agent say? "Okay, that's no problem. If I understand you correctly, you're not absolutely sure this is the right home for you, and you don't want to buy unless you are certain, is that right?"

Pin down the prospect. "In other words, if it weren't for _____, you would buy/list, is that correct?"

No matter the objection, this track works. And even if you can't handle the stated objection, you'll sound terrific responding to it.

SHOW AND SELL WITH VISUALS

Show and sell your way over the objection. Remember the buyer who was turned off by the damaged driveway? Start step four by saying, "I'd like to show you something that will help you make a decision. Correct me if I'm wrong, but you feel that if you have to replace the driveway, you'll be spending too much money for the home, is that right? Is that your only objection to buying this home today? I'd like to show you something which will help you make a decision."

What would you show? Maybe one of a hundred different visuals. The attempt will get you a lot farther than anything you actually tell or show the prospect. Perhaps with the multi-listings book, you could show the buyer there are other homes with driveways in better condition. But one of two things will result. Either some of the features of the current selection must be sacrificed, or the buyer must pay more.

In effect, purchasing the home with the damaged driveway gets the buyer all the home he or she wants at a lower price. And if you think you couldn't convince anyone of this, you're costing yourself a fortune. You might think, "Well, it wouldn't convince me." But you aren't paying your commission. Your prospects are doing that. They're the people who must be convinced.

Most techniques don't work most of the time. That's why you must learn as many as possible. The more, the better. Suppose you're discussing with a potential seller the possibility of listing, and the seller says, "We're not really sure we want to list. Another broker said we could get more money."

First, agree. "I can certainly understand how you might feel about getting every possible nickel which you can from the sale of your lovely home." Then, feed back. "Are you saying that the other broker proved that you could get more money, using facts as I did? Or did the broker simply say you could get more money? Which was it?"

"Well, he said so," comes the reply.

Step three, isolate the objection. "Would you list with me tonight at this marketable price if I could prove to you that listing at a higher price could destroy your plans to move?" Assuming they would, go to step four—show and sell with visuals. You might produce a copy of a market analysis or a multi-listings book.

"I would like to show you something that may help you make a decision. My recommended price was determined by comparing your home with similar homes sold recently and listed in this market analysis. As you agreed earlier, your home should only sell on today's market at what buyers are paying for comparable homes."

"But I didn't show you this other section of the market analysis— the part we call the expired listings. Believe me, I certainly understand how you could want more money for this charming home. And if you could get it, I would benefit by getting a better commission, too."

"All of these homeowners in the expired column felt exactly the same way you do right now. They wanted to put their homes on the market at just a little more money, based on hearsay. But the majority of these homeowners found that they had to cancel their plans to move, because their homes were not sold. I don't think cancelling your move is really what you want to do, is it? So if you'll just give me your okay right there, please? And by the way, press hard, would you? This is cheap carbon."

This particular technique has been around since the beginning of time. And it's the most helpful technique I have found to keep a seller from listing at a higher price.

Step one, agree with them. In this case, the seller had an objection. It was logical. Anyone would want the best price he or she could get.

Step two, understand the objection. Then feed it back so it will give the prospect something to consider. Meanwhile, the agent gets time to think. In this case, the agent chose to use the feedback statement to challenge the other agent's credibility.

What should you use as criteria for determining which words to use? The prospect, the situation and what you might have said before. Don't be concerned with the words as much as the concepts and actual steps of the track. In a live situation with a prospect, I haven't the slightest idea what words I will use. All I know are the steps. If a person is comfortable with those, the words will come automatically and naturally.

Step three, ask the isolation question. The purpose is to get the prospect to commit a decision or admit there are other objections.

Step four, visual and verbiage. Show the prospect anything that might help bring about a decision. And don't think it won't work if you wouldn't believe it. You must try; if you don't, the sale ends here, and you lose.

But if you try, the attempt itself often will carry more weight with the prospect than the actual solution. What would convince you is not important; you're not going to list or buy. Your prospects are. They're the ones to convince. There are so many different ways to do it, too. Your job is to choose the method you believe will have the most impact on your prospect.

Step five, ask the closing question. Assume they saw the logic in step four. Even if they didn't understand, they might be too embarrassed to admit it. Don't talk yourself out of a sale.

When the prospects said they didn't want to cancel their plans, they actually were setting you up to wrap up the transaction. So let me close this chapter by giving you a magic closing question. It's one of the softest, yet most powerful, closing questions you can ask. It's so powerful that I call this question Moneymaker No. 3.

The question? "Any questions?"

Think about this one. The prospects have just stated an objection, and you've talked your way through it. Then you ask, "Any questions?" If they have more questions, then answer them. And if they don't, that means they should be ready to make a decision, and there's only one thing left to do.

Close.

IN A CAPSULE

1. Learn how to close. A big part of the people business requires getting prospects to make decisions with which they aren't comfortable.

2. You must work at developing closing skills. Practice, drill and rehearse the steps of a closing track designed to sell the prospect.

3. There are no foolproof methods for handling stalls and objections. There are scores of techniques for handling them, because people are complex and different. Learn as many techniques as possible.

4. Adopt an "Oh, well, that didn't work" attitude. It will keep you in a better frame of mind when trying to cope with objections and stalls.

5. Remember, an objection is the real reason for a prospect not to take action. A stall is the reason the prospect gives which differs from the real reason.

6. Objections boil down to three reasons—money, lack of confidence or fear. Learn how to handle all three.

7. A condition is a prospect's reason for not taking action that the agent cannot control. But conditions can change. A new job or a promotion can turn a nonbuyer into a buyer overnight.

8. There are four times to handle stalls and objections— never, later, as they occur and before they occur. Know when to handle what stall or objection.

9. The objection and stall handling track consists of five steps—agreement, feedback, isolation, visual and verbiage (show and sell) and closing. Know what each step

entails. Don't be concerned so much with the words you will use as with the concept behind each step.

10. Remember Moneymaker No. 3—the magic closing question: "Any questions?"

List the most important points you have gained from the
preceding Strategy:

_____

_____

_____

_____

_____

_____

_____

_____

_____

_____

_____

_____

_____

_____

_____

_____

_____

_____

NOTES

Section 4

CLOSING THE DEAL

11

Close, Close and Close Again

My first year in real estate was lousy. It was so bad, I thought a closing was when you were on from six to nine at night and were responsible for locking the doors.

I was my own worst enemy. Whenever I heard a technique, I would always think, "I can't see how that would work, because I would never be persuaded by it."

Finally, it dawned on me that I don't have to be persuaded by it. I'm not the seller. It's up to other people to decide whether to be persuaded by it, and since paying my bills depends on their decisions to buy and sell, I decided that I'd better get into the business of convincing.

That helped me develop the attitude of, "Oh, well, that didn't work. I'd better try something else." In time, I found that attitude was far superior to the attitude of, "Darn, that didn't work. What do I do now? Go home I guess."

LET'S LOOK AROUND

A typical objection real estate salespeople hear is, "Maybe I should look at some other homes before making a decision." How do you deal with that one?

Let's set the scene. Mr. and Mrs. Prospect call an agent after seeing an advertisement. The agent motivates them to come into the office. Agent and prospects establish a rapport, and the agent takes control. The prospects are qualified, the agent demonstrates properties and finds a house that is simply perfect for the prospects, in comparison with everything else that's currently on the market.

The agent simply knows the prospects should buy this home. But the agent also knows, through experience, that if the prospects don't buy this home, they may never find another as good at the same price. So the agent has an obligation to keep selling, even when prospects object.

Let's take a closer look. Here's a simulated exercise which helps an agent to always be on track. That's the important thing. Don't concern yourself with the words as much as the concept behind them. By understanding the concepts and staying on track, you'll decrease your chances of being "derailed."

AGENT: Mr. and Mrs. Prospect, I certainly appreciate the time you spent this afternoon to come to my office and let me review these papers with you. Do you have any questions on anything that we've discussed so far?

PROSPECT: No, I don't think so.

AGENT: Well, if you have no questions, Mr. Prospect, I'll need your signature right there. Now press hard, it's cheap carbon. And Mrs. Prospect, would you sign on that next line? By the way, get all six copies, would you please?

PROSPECT: Well, I think we're going to buy the house. But before we do, we'd like to look at some other homes.

AGENT: All right. As far as I'm concerned, that's no problem at all. I certainly can understand how you wouldn't want to buy a home unless you were absolutely sure that you've seen enough selections. If I understand what you're saying, looking at one or two other homes might make you feel more comfortable about making a decision on this home that you like so much. Is that the only thing preventing you from buying this home today?

PROSPECT: Yes, it is.

AGENT: Okay. I'd like to show you something if I can that may help you make a decision. In other words, whether you buy the home today, tomorrow, the next day or whenever makes no difference at all to me. You're my customer, and whatever you decide is fine with me. But I just wouldn't want to see you make a mistake that we all might regret later. So let me show you something that may help you decide. Is that all right?

PROSPECT: Sure.

AGENT: Here's a copy of the multi-listings book again. Let's review what we've done so far. First, we talked about your finances. And I think we've narrowed it down to a home in this area. And I think we've narrowed it down to a price with which you're comfortable, is that right?

PROSPECT: That's right.

AGENT: Okay, and we checked the current listings and narrowed your possibilities down to the selection that we have. So what you're saying is, that maybe—just maybe—there's another home out there that might be even better. Is that right?

PROSPECT: Well, that's what we were thinking. . . .

AGENT: Okay, let's go through this multi-listings book again. Here's the one we're considering now. This one is your home. It is nice, isn't it?

PROSPECT: Yes.

AGENT: Here's one we didn't see. This is on Shady Lane. But you notice that this particular home doesn't have that extra room you wanted for sewing, Mrs. Prospect. And I thought that was important to you, wasn't it?

PROSPECT: It is.

AGENT: Okay, let's see what else we have. Here's another home, and it's got the same qualities as your selection. As a matter of fact, if you notice here, it even has a patio area, which your home doesn't have. But if you'll also notice, they want more money for this home. You definitely need three bedrooms, right? You couldn't get along with only two, right?

PROSPECT: That's right.

AGENT: Okay, these are the other homes that are available. We know you like your selection. Right or wrong?

PROSPECT: Right.

AGENT: We know that you can afford the home, and we also know that I can find you another home. That would be no problem. But the way it appears, one of two things will happen. You'll either give up some of the features

216

that you like so much in this selection, or you'll pay more. So I think we've found the right home, didn't we?

PROSPECT: I think we did.

AGENT: Then I'm going to need your okay. Press hard, it's cheap carbon. And get all six copies, so the signature will be legible on your copy, okay?

Sounds familiar, doesn't it? Remember the man with the disaster area for a driveway. He had a different problem, but the agent's strategy is the same in both cases. This couple felt that they hadn't looked around enough. But the agent convinced both sets of buyers that they had indeed found the right homes by boiling down their complaints to their common denominators—sacrifice. The buyers either must sacrifice desired features or pay more for a similar home in a better location or with a better driveway.

In both cases, the agent used simple logic. Buyers may look forever and never find two homes exactly alike. They're like snowflakes, remember?

Understand the process. The agent asked for the prospects' signatures. The prospects didn't feel comfortable, so they stated an objection. That's not a stall. An objection is the real reason for not making a decision. In this case, the prospects felt they hadn't seen enough homes to make an intelligent decision. They believed if they looked at others, they might be able to find a better home.

So the agent's strategy in dealing with the objection is simple: Step one, agree. Step two, feed back the objection. Step three, isolate the objection. Step four, show and sell, using simple logic. Then step five, go for the close. That's what takes intestinal fortitude. But you'll notice the agent kept the closing soft, saying, "I think we've found the right home, didn't we?"

There are no bad closing questions. The agent might have said, "Well, that answers that, doesn't it?" or, "That makes a difference, doesn't it?'' Or, the agent may have simply said, ''Any questions?'' The point is, the agent won over the prospects by getting a commitment. Then the agent did the only thing left to be done—hand the buyers a pen.

The agent has a responsibility to close. Also, most of the money made in the real estate business comes when agents close, close and close again. When you stay on track with persistence, you'll be amazed at how much more money you will earn in less time and with less effort.

THE "ATTORNEY" OBJECTION

Another common objection real estate agents hear is ''I want to take the papers to my attorney before I sign anything.'' Prospects aren't always comfortable making decisions. Sometimes, they just want to be sure that everything is legitimate and that their interests are protected. So they tell the agent, ''I want to talk to my attorney first.''

Let's detail this objection, along with the agent's method of handling it.

> **AGENT:** Okay, Mr. and Mrs. Prospect, I certainly appreciate the extra time you took to come back to the office so I could go through all these details with you. Do you have any questions about anything that we've talked about so far?

> **PROSPECT:** No.

> **AGENT:** Then I'll need your okay right here on this purchase form. Now press hard, it's cheap carbon. And by the way, get all six copies. . . .

PROSPECT: Before we sign, we'd like to have our attorney look at these papers, if you don't mind.

AGENT: Sure, it's entirely your decision, and I can certainly understand how you might want an attorney to see the forms. But I'm a little surprised that you'd want to do this prematurely. If I understand exactly what you're saying, you want the attorney to look at the forms to make sure everything is legal, so you don't get into some sort of a bind. Is that correct?

PROSPECT: Absolutely.

AGENT: I'd just like to show you something that may help you make a decision. May I take just a minute on this? This purchase form was prepared by a group of attorneys. If you don't know this, it's probably my fault for not telling you. You've heard a lot about consumer protection recently, haven't you? And there are perhaps certain legal words in this form that your attorney should read, but not necessarily prematurely. Does your attorney normally charge for consultation?

PROSPECT: Of course.

AGENT: And you want your attorney to check out the legality of the contract, is that correct?

PROSPECT: That's right.

AGENT: In other words, you can make your own decision on the price, right?

PROSPECT: Right.

AGENT: And we know what the down payment is, don't we. And as for the deposit, right here it reads, "In the event of default by the seller hereunder, we will return your deposit to you.'' So deposit also isn't a problem, right?

PROSPECT: That's right.

AGENT: That leaves possession, and right here, it says, ''The seller will vacate the property sixty days after the time of closing or settlement, or they will pay rental fee in the amount of $20 per day.'' That's equal to your monthly payment, so there's no question on that, is there?

PROSPECT: No.

AGENT: Then probably the only area your attorney would investigate is title insurance. And the contract states that in the event the title is not marketable, based upon an opinion by the purchaser's attorney, the purchasers' deposit shall be refunded. A lot of buyers don't realize that the title insurance isn't ready for an attorney's inspection until just prior to closing. So I wouldn't want to see you go to an attorney and have to pay a consultation fee to okay something that's not applicable now. And it says right here that if the attorney doesn't deem the title to be marketable, you don't have to buy the home, and you don't lose a nickel of your deposit. So this should save you a few bucks with your attorney. Any questions? (Remember, this is Moneymaker No. 3.)

PROSPECT: No.

AGENT: Okay, I'll need your okay, right there. And by the way, press hard, it's cheap carbon. . . .

How many purchasers do you think actually have an attorney of their own? Very few. In fact, how many were actually advised to show the papers to an attorney before they sign. Perhaps one or two out of ten. The odds are small enough that when buyers say they want to consult with their attorneys, they generally must find one. Then they must pay attorney fees.

I can appreciate a purchaser wanting to consult with an attorney. There are certain legal complications with every offer to purchase. But taking the papers to an attorney before the sale is made is premature. After all, the buyer knows more than the attorney about the price of the home. The buyer also knows more about whether he or she qualifies for the home than the attorney. The buyer knows more than the attorney about what's included or excluded from the sale.

The major concern of the attorney is the wording of the purchase agreement. Is it correct? Of course, it is, because a group of attorneys wrote it. So that means that the real job of the attorney is to determine whether the title is marketable. And there is no way in the world an attorney can determine if the title is marketable until just prior to the closing or settlement.

(WARNING: An exception to this advice would involve complicated transactions or those involving unusual terms. In such cases, a buyer's consultation with an attorney should be encouraged before the contract is signed.)

So how did the agent handle the buyer's objection. Again, the agent used logic, which again boils down to sacrifice. Prospects may do anything they want, but it will cost them. That's the thrust of the track—to make the seller or buyer aware that it's costly to hesitate.

There is no magic in tracks. All you do is simply use a visual, along with simple logic, to illustrate a point. By learning to do this, you'll amaze yourself at how adept you'll become at handling and overcoming objections. And you'll be surprised at how the process will make prospects more comfortable about deciding right away.

It's called closing. If prospects object, give them a little more information, then close again. It doesn't always work. Nothing does. You just keep trying until the prospect signs on the dotted line.

How many times should you close? That's up to you. I once

heard a trainer suggest fifty times, as many as it takes to get the sale. I don't know anyone who has that firm of a resolve. I certainly don't.

But there is magic in three's. And if you can just commit yourself to close, close and close again, you'll increase your overall sales. And if you think it sounds like I'm trying to sell you on this, you're right. I am. This is what works, and finding out what works is why you bought this book.

THE LOW OFFER

Let's discuss another typical objection agents often hear—a seller thinks an offer is too low. An agent has received a bona fide offer from the buyer. At this point, the agent must present the offer to the seller.

Under no circumstances should the agent present the offer to the seller via telephone. If the seller doesn't like the offer, it will be harder for the agent to persuade the seller to accept the offer over the telephone than it would be if agent and seller were in a face-to-face situation.

Instead, the agent should make an appointment with the seller. If the seller asks how much the offer is, the agent should respond by saying that discussions still are under way with the buyer. Then an appointment should be scheduled.

When the agent arrives, he or she should discuss fully the offer with the seller. The conversation may go something like this:

AGENT: Do you have any questions at all on what we've gone over so far, Mr. and Mrs. Seller?

SELLER: No, we don't.

AGENT: Okay, then let me have your copies, I'm going to need your okay right here, and press hard, this is cheap. . . .

SELLER: We've talked this over, and the offer really is not quite as much as we expected.

AGENT: Well, I certainly understand that. And I realize when I came in this evening that it isn't exactly what we've had in mind. So let me reassure you that I don't blame you for not wanting to take less for this beautiful home. Now let me see if I understand exactly what you're saying. There's nothing wrong with any of the other details; the offer is just too low. Is that right?

SELLER: That's right.

AGENT: Okay, Mr. Seller, how low is it?

SELLER: Two thousand dollars.

AGENT: Do you feel the same way, Mrs. Seller?

SELLER: Yes.

AGENT: Other than the $2,000, is there anything else preventing you from selling tonight?

SELLER: No.

AGENT: All right. I'd like to show you something, if I can. It would only take a couple of minutes, and this may help prevent you from making the wrong decision. Would that be all right?

SELLER: Sure.

AGENT: Rest assured that I would rather sell your home for more money than less money, and that's not just for your sake, although that would give me great satisfaction. But the amount of my commission is directly related to the selling price of the home. You understand that, don't you? So we're in this thing together. But let's look at this situation in its worst light. Let's pretend, for the sake of argument, that there's no way in the world you can get the extra $2,000. What's the worst thing that could happen? You would have $2,000 less to put on your new home. Is that right?

SELLER: That's right.

AGENT: And at worst, if you didn't have the $2,000, you would be forced to get a little higher mortgage on your new home. True?

SELLER: True.

AGENT: All right. There is a table called an amortization book, or a payment schedule. What's the interest rate you'll be getting on your new home?

SELLER: The current rate.

AGENT: Okay, let's go to the page with that percent of interest. Now this would be a twenty-year mortgage, right?

SELLER: That's right.

AGENT: Let's just pretend that you had to spend $2,000 more. That will amount to approximately $26 more per month than you would pay with the extra $2,000. Do you follow me so far?

SELLER: I follow you.

AGENT: Okay. I just don't want to see you make a mistake. If you look at the situation realistically, the extra $26 per month amounts only to about eighty-five cents per day. Don't gamble. You must ask yourself, is it worth eighty-five cents per day to gamble on losing the new

home? I don't think it's worth eighty-five cents per day,
is it?

SELLER: I see what you mean.

AGENT: Okay, then I'm going to need your okay right
here. And press hard. . . .

The agent did something that you probably do to yourself—the
old "break-it-down-to-the-minimum" close. It's also been around
since the beginning of time. I remember the first time I ever heard
that close. I said, "Oh, how could you do that? How could you
take their $2,000 and break it all the way down to eighty-five cents
per day?" Simple. It's mathematically correct.

That close is so logical, it's pathetic that some agents can't or
won't relate to it. It's like buying a new car. The dealer talks you
into buying a model with a sunroof. It may cost an extra $1,000.
But you buy it because you want it. It's only an extra dollar per
day. And the sunroof will contribute to the resale value.

Or you may have gone to a department store and seen a refrigerator
that you wanted. You also saw the ones that sold for a few dollars
more, all the way up to a few hundred dollars more. And if you
decided you wanted the one that cost more, you'd break it down to
the minimum in your own mind.

This technique still boils down to the same factor as the others—
impress upon the client that hesitating can force sacrifices. In this
case, the seller was gambling eighty-five cents per day on holding
out. If he had lost the gamble, he could have wound up either not
making a sale at the price he wanted, or making one too late to
qualify for the current interest rate.

All of these hypothetical situations were handled the same way—
by staying on track. When you stay on track, you help people see
the risks they can be taking by waiting, hesitating or refusing to
take action.

Just remember: If you can't close, you can't sell.

AN OFFER YOU MUST REFUSE

Of course, convincing the seller to accept a low offer may not be the most prudent course of action. Suppose the buyer's offer is so ridiculously low that you know the seller won't entertain any possibility of accepting it. If and when that happens, you'll need a technique to bring your buyer back down to earth.

So let me offer you a technique from noted real estate negotiator/speaker/trainer, Roger Dawson, author of *You Can Get Anything You Want*. When a buyer makes a ridiculously low offer, the agent has but to ask two questions and make one statement:

1. Is that offer the best you can do? (If the buyer says no, then get another, more serious offer. But more than likely, the buyer will say yes. Then you ask the second question.)

2. You are serious about acquiring this property, aren't you? (The buyer will most definitely say yes. Then make your statement.)

3. Then you'll have to do better than that.

This technique will produce favorable results most of the time, and most of the time is good odds in this business. In fact, for your own personal information, this technique works well in reverse. When you are buying something that requires negotiation and a price is quoted, you can use this technique against the salesperson. Just change the word "offer" to "price" in the first question and "acquiring" to "selling" in the second question (and substitute whatever it is you're buying for the word "property," of course) and you'll have a good negotiating weapon.

IN A CAPSULE

1. Don't be concerned if you think certain techniques wouldn't convince you. They don't have to convince you, because you aren't paying your commissions. If you don't try techniques on prospects because you assume the techniques would never convince them, you're costing yourself a fortune.

2. An agent must convince a hesitant prospect that not taking action means sacrifices of some type. Usually, the longer a prospect waits to take action, the more it will cost.

3. If a buyer doesn't want to buy a selected home, even though you know it's the best home available for the buyer's money, stress that more house will cost more money.

4. If a prospect wants to take the transaction papers to an attorney before signing, convince the prospect that such action now is unnecessary and costly. The papers won't be ready for an attorney's inspection until just prior to the closing.

5   If a seller refuses a low offer, break the difference down to the minimum. For example, if an offer is $2,000 less than the asking price, break it down to a daily price, computed over the basis of a twenty-year mortgage. In this case, it would amount to about eighty-five cents per day.

6. When you receive a ridiculously low offer, bring the buyer back down to earth by asking if the offer is the best the buyer can do. Then ask if the buyer is serious about acquiring the property. If he or she is serious, tell the buyer that he or she will simply have to do better. It's a good technique that works a majority of the time.

List the most important points you have gained from the
preceding Strategy:

_____

_____

_____

_____

_____

_____

_____

_____

_____

_____

_____

_____

_____

_____

_____

_____

_____

_____

12

Negotiating with the Seller

While serving as a trainer for a group of real estate offices several years ago, I met a saleswoman who had just written a $68,000 offer on a listing priced at $72,000. It sounded pretty good to me. If ever there was an offer that should have been accepted, or at least counter-offered, this was it.

The saleswoman was elated. The listing was her own, which meant she would earn a double commission if she sold the home— one for the listing itself and one for the actual sale. That's called a "double-dip" in the real estate business. Making the sale would have added more than $2,000 to her pocketbook.

She grabbed her briefcase and was on her way out of the door when I asked her, "Are you prepared? Do you have everything you need?"

"I don't think I'll need anything," she replied.

I tried to persuade her to take a few minutes to prepare a market analysis and an estimate of the seller's net profit, but to no avail. The woman left the office with dollar signs in her eyes.

Thirty minutes later she came back, minus the dollar signs. She took the written offer out of her briefcase. On it was written the word, "REJECTED."

I almost fell flat on the floor. I couldn't believe that agent was so close to earning approximately $2,000 in commissions, yet she wouldn't take the time to make the necessary preparations for getting the offer accepted.

LEARN FROM EXPERIENCE

The best way to learn about real estate is from experience—other people's experience. So learn from this woman's misfortune (which, incidentally, she brought on herself.)

There are a few simple steps an agent can take to improve the odds of the offer being accepted. And considering that these steps can make the difference between earning and losing the commission, they are certainly worth the little time they require.

1. *Estimate the seller's total expenses and net revenue, and prepare a market analysis—before you leave your office.* This will prove to the seller that other similar homes in the market have sold for similar prices. Also, know facts and financial information about the buyer, and list any positive factors about the buyer which may impress the seller.

2. *Choose your ground.* There is a right and a wrong place to capture the seller's attention when presenting an offer. For example, let's say you believe the best place to

present the offer is at the seller's residence, late in the evening while the children are asleep. Be sure when you call to present the offer to let the seller know you want to come over then.

3. *Join forces with the seller.* If you start talking about "My buyer wants this," and "My buyer wants that," you run the risk of alienating the seller. This will give the impression that you and the buyer are working against the seller. Too many times, I've sat across tables from co-workers who brought offers on my listings. They would talk incessantly about their buyers, then wonder why the sellers declined their offers. When negotiating, sellers want to think the agent is on their side.

   For example, suppose you go to present an offer. Instead of referring to the buyer as "My buyer," you might say, "I just want you to know that the buyers certainly are impressed with the way you take care of your home, and they wanted me to be sure to tell you." Then use the "we" concept. Explain to the seller that you have an offer, and "we" have to look at the facts, and then "we" have to find a way not to lose "our" buyer. Join forces with the sellers. Don't sell against them. You won't sell without them.

4. *Be clear whenever you negotiate.* There is much more to an offer tnan just price. Too often, agents talk in extremely technical terms that confuse most people. Suppose you have a buyer who makes an assumption offer. The buyer plans to take over the existing payments. You could say to the seller, "We have a buyer who want to purchase your home at $75,000 and assume your mortgage balance, which means the buyer will take over your principle and interest, including your mortgage insurance premiun And by the way, tney will reimburse you your escrow and etc."

When people are confused, they can't make comfortable and rational decisions. Make the offer clear. Sellers primarily are interested in three basic questions and answers.

- How much in-pocket cash will they get?
- When will they get it?
- Will the sale go through?

To keep it clear for the seller, don't read the offer until you answer those three questions. Tell them that, based on your information, you can help the seller realize, at the time of closing, "X" amount of in-pocket dollars, and that he or she will receive it in "X" number of days. And assure them there is very little risk of the sale falling through because you personally qualified the buyer.

5. *Get decisions on minor points first.* If you have an offer that's less than full price and terms, handle minor details before you discuss price. For example, "The buyers expressed an interest in your work bench in the basement, and they wanted me to be sure and ask if, in the event we work out the details tonight, there would be anything preventing you from leaving it behind." Then write down the answer.

Discuss any points on possession which the seller may not understand. For example, "If we can work out the details with this buyer, you'll be able to stay in the home for sixty days. Will that be enough?"

Work out little details first when negotiating. Just like with questions and "yeses," if you get a lot of little agreements, getting the bigger agreements will be much easier.

6. *Create an attitude of proposal.* Too often, buyers make an offer. The agent takes the offer to the seller, who

accepts it. Agent calls buyer and says, "Congratulations. You've just bought a home." And the buyer hedges, expressing an interest in looking around some more.

Never let a buyer feel that all details have been properly handled. If the buyers leave your office thinking they've bought a home, there is only one thing left for them to think—how to back out.

Send the buyers home after planting a "Gee-I-hope-this-works-out" attitude in their minds. And this is applicable even if you have a full price offer. You might say, "I'm going to present this offer to the seller, and, of course, I'm not sure whether or not the seller will accept. It might be a couple of hours before I can present the offer, and there are so many people in our multi-listing area. Another buyer in the meantime could look at the house and decide to buy it. That probably won't happen, but it could. So you go on home now, and I'll call you. Keep your fingers crossed."

Then call the buyers in a few hours and say, "Congratulations, you've just bought a home." If you handle it this way, you'll increase your odds of having the buyers react by saying, "Well, this is good news. We're glad somebody else didn't buy it."

Even if the offer is accepted, you should create an attitude of proposal with the seller. If you don't and something should fall through, you'll be the bad guy. When you leave the seller, say, "I want to thank you for accepting this offer, and I don't think we're making a mistake. The important thing is selling your home. But let me share this with you: Anything could happen. There's a possibility that (in case of a new mortgage sale) the home won't appraise high enough. Or maybe the buyer has some problems on his credit report that I haven't been told. These things probably won't happen, but keep your fingers crossed."

PROBING DEEPER

Now let's go back and discuss each point even further.

Rule No. 1—Prepare. Suppose you have an offer that's lower than full price and terms. What specifically would you want to prepare to show the seller? Beside the items listed earlier, you would want to show the seller a list of comparable homes which have sold in the area, preferably since the seller's home was listed. The seller may accept the offer without seeing this list, but you never know. It's like the parachute in an airplane. It's not important to the pilot until the plane develops trouble. It doesn't hurt to carry it along.

Rule No. 2—Choose your ground. Once I wrote and presented an offer all in one sitting. I showed a home located miles away from the office. Both buyers and sellers were present. Everybody got along well, so we all sat at the dining room table and negotiated the sale right there, and everybody signed the proper papers. But the odds of something like that happening at all are very slim.

Always try to see the seller at his or her home after the children are asleep. This will give you a better chance to hold the seller's attention. In the case of a counter-offer, try to motivate the buyer to come back to your office.

Rule No. 3—Join forces with the sellers. Let the sellers know that if "we" don't accept this particular offer, "we" go all the way back to square one. Remember to use the "we" concept in presenting the offer to the seller.

Rule No. 4—Be clear when you negotiate. Place your offer in a file folder, upon which you can write down all the key points to the offer, such as the net figure, occupancy date and certain other items to include or exclude to give the seller an overview of what to expect.

Rule No. 5—Get decisions on minor points first. Remember, agreements on the little things make it easier to get agreement on the major point.

Rule No. 6—Create an attitude of proposal. Keep both seller and buyer on the edge of their chairs. It's good salesmanship, and it increases the odds of getting a commission.

SMALL TALK

Do you think that small talk can help prime a seller to accept an offer? Sure it can, if it really isn't small talk at all. When presenting an offer to a seller, pre-plan your small talk. There are three things that would be good to discuss with sellers to get them in the proper frame of mind.

1. *Market conditions.* Tell the seller how hard you had to work to land the buyer. Point out that the market is a bit tighter than agents would like. Why would you talk so negatively to a seller? To get the seller in the proper frame of mind.

2. *The seller's plans.* "How's your new house coming along?" is a good question to ask. Suppose the answer is, "It will be ready in about two months." Then you can counter with, "Well, that doesn't give us much time, does it?" Remind the sellers of their plans. That, too, will help get them thinking properly.

3. *The buyer.* Get the seller to like the buyer. Sometimes, sellers will bend on price if they like the buyers. So

you might say, "You had a chance to meet the buyers when I showed them the home last Sunday. What did you think of them? Isn't their little girl beautiful?" Then you might pay a compliment on behalf of the buyers. "Mrs. Buyer certainly did like the decor in your dining room, and I promised them I would pass that comment on to you."

Break the ice with not-so-small talk. Then go to the minor details. Will they leave the rose bushes? If so, fine. If not, that's fine, too. Keep it upbeat. Just tell the sellers you promised the buyers you would at least ask.

PRESENT THE OFFER

Reach into your briefcase and get the file folder with the offer and other information. But before you hand it to the sellers, detail their options. They have three.

- Accept the offer.
- Reject the offer.
- Make a counter offer (which constitutes a rejection).

Stage a short presentation, borrowing salt and pepper shakers and an ashtray, if possible, and use them to demonstrate what you will say next:

"Let me explain my job. There are three ingredients for a successful sale—a seller, a buyer and a house. And we have all three. My job is to present to you the buyer's proposal. And you have three choices:

"Option one: You can accept the buyer's proposal, and we have a sale. Option two: You can reject the proposal, and we don't have a sale. And option three: You can counter propose on the buyer's proposal, which, I warn you, also constitutes a rejection.

"If you choose options two or three, we go back to square one as far as the buyer is concerned. As we go through the details, all I want you to do is carefully consider everything, because I don't want to see us go back to square one."

Why explain this in advance? You don't want them to be their own worst enemies by rejecting an offer that they really should accept.

HIGHLIGHT THE OFFER

Give the sellers the details of the buyer's offer—the in-pocket cash, estimated time the sellers will get it and how much of a risk there is about the sale going through. For example, you might say, "Based on my information at the closing, you will walk away with $24,200 in your pocket, and you'll have your money in sixty days. But most importantly, in my opinion, you'll have a strong buyer. If you accept the offer, you can relax and start planning your move."

Now it's time to read the purchase agreement, regardless of whether they accepted or rejected the offer. Actually, they can't make a rational decision without knowing all the facts. And if you've expressed yourself in a fashion that would appeal to the seller's sense of logic, chances are good that they will accept.

IN A CAPSULE

1. Improve your odds of selling a listing by taking six steps:
   (a) Estimate the seller's expenses and net income.
   (b) Choose your ground for negotiation. You need to be in control.
   (c) Join forces with the seller. Don't alienate the seller by talking incessantly about "your" buyer. Use the "we" concept when negotiating.
   (d) Be clear when you negotiate. Keep it simple for the seller.
   (e) Get decisions on minor points first. The more "yeses" you can get on minor points, the easier it will be to get a "yes" on the major points.
   (f) Create an attitude of proposal. Always leave a buyer and a seller hoping the sale will go through. If you leave a buyer convinced that the sale will go through, the buyer may change his or her mind. If you leave a seller with the feeling that the house has definitely been sold, then the sale falls through, the seller will blame you.

2. Small talk is fine, as long as it isn't really small. Set the stage for negotiations with the seller by discussing market conditions, the seller's plans and the buyer.

3. When presenting an offer, give the seller the options in advance. This way, the seller knows exactly what steps to take. This keeps the negotiations clear.

List the most important points you have gained from the
preceding Strategy:

_____

_____

_____

_____

_____

_____

_____

_____

_____

_____

_____

_____

_____

_____

_____

_____

_____

13

Negotiating with the Buyer

Have you ever lost a buyer in your office parking lot? How frustrating! The buyers came into your office to be qualified, and you carefully selected three to four properties to demonstrate. The last house seemed to be the favorite, and you and the buyers return to the office to talk business.

All of a sudden, the buyers leave. Seems that they have an unexpected funeral to attend, or some urgent grocery shopping to do. This is what is known as the old parking lot routine, and it happens to the average agent more than he or she would admit.

The reason the buyers tell you they are leaving is not important. What is important is the strong possibility that if they leave, you may never see them again. So if you want to save that commission, you'd better find a way to stop them.

And pistols are out. Even though Willie Sutton thought a lot of their power to persuade, they don't calm nervous buyers, and it's terrible for public relations!

If there is indeed a buyer's training school, that's the number one technique that is taught. The buyers tell the agent that they like the house, but they'll call him back later. Too many real estate agents return to the office alone after showing "the right home" to a qualified buyer, believing the buyer really will call back.

Most of the time, though, the buyer doesn't call. And if a qualified buyer disappears after touring "the right home," odds are pretty good that he or she won't buy the house.

IT'S A MATTER OF NERVES

Buyers are nervous. They're considering a multi-thousand-dollar investment. It's not easy.

Remember the last car you bought? Did you not get at least a little nervous? Anytime you commit yourself to forty-eight months of $200 or so payments, your palms tend to perspire. So how do you think a prospective home buyer feels signing away thirty years of several hundred dollars per month? Giddy? No. Nerves are ripping the buyer's stomach to shreds.

Some people have to think for days before they buy anything. Something as small in comparison as a television set or a refrigerator often require major conferences between husband and wife, as if it were one of life's biggest purchases.

Potential home buyers seek the sanctuary of their comfortable worlds where the pressure isn't bearing upon them to make decisions. Unfortunately, they will never feel at ease about making that multi-thousand-dollar purchase (unless a rich uncle dies). So they often decide not to decide. Forever. Or at least until they find an agent who can talk them out of leaving the parking lot.

And that can be you, because you're going to show them— before they leave the parking lot—that you understand their nervousness. Remember, the best time to handle some objections is before they even come up. The buyers haven't told you they're nervous. But it doesn't take a mind-reader to know that they are.

BE SMOOTH

Use your most calming tone of voice. If you don't, there will be three uptight people in the car, and that's no good. As relaxed as you possibly can be, tell the buyers you understand they might be nervous because they're not sure whether they want to commit themselves. Then ask them to come into your office so you at least can answer any questions they have about the home.

Perhaps they won't have any more questions, but they'll still want to leave. So then, you might say, "Let me at least prepare all the facts, as if you had agreed to buy. That way, whatever you decide will be a more logical decision.

"Then, one or two things will happen. You'll buy the home, which I hope would make you happy, or you won't buy it. This way, if you don't buy it, at least I won't have to worry about why I lost the sale. If I know that you weighed everything in your minds before making the decision, I'll feel better about having served you properly."

If an agent said that to me, I'd go into the office. But you don't really care what I'd do. Instead, you probably want to know what to do if the second approach doesn't work.

If that approach fails, ask the buyers if they would purchase the home for $10,000 less than the asking price. That should lure them inside. Of course, you won't be able to knock ten grand off the asking price. The seller would put his Doberman on you if you even asked. But once you get the buyers into the office, you can probably get back the $10,000, $2,000 at a time.

Well, it's better than losing the buyers in the parking lot, isn't it? And if that approach doesn't work, then you may use your pistol.

Of course, that's in jest. But if you know what to say and when and how to say it, you'll find that words are the best weapons you could ever use.

THE BASIC CLOSE

Once you get your buyers into your office, show them to chairs located away from any hustle and bustle that may be in session. Offer them soft drinks or coffee. The purchase agreement and buyer's financial statement are before you, if you need them. You also have a line pad, a copy of the listing agreement and any other forms that are pertinent to selling a home.

Now it's time for the basic close. It's a three-step process.

1. *Discuss and iron out the details.* Before you can start preparing any purchase agreement, be sure the details are clearly understood. For example, will the seller repair the driveway? Are the draperies included with the house? When do the buyers get possession? All of these points must be discussed with the buyer immediately.

2. *Recap their down payment and financial monthly installments.* Before you receive anything, be sure that both you and the buyers understand all the facts. Once that is done, prepare the purchase agreement.

3. *Read the purchase agreement to the buyers.* Give a copy to each person, and keep one for yourself. Ask the buyers to follow as you read and to stop you if there is any point they don't understand.

Let's look more closely at step two. No one has said anything about purchasing. Yet, you're filling out a purchase agreement. Isn't that a bit premature? Seventy percent of all real estate agents think so.

Suppose a qualified buyer was considering a particular house. And suppose the buyer said to you, "I'm not sure at all that I'm going to buy this house. But would you mind very much typing up all the papers and filling out the preliminary purchase agreements for me? Once I read them, I can decide either 'yes' or 'no.' "

Would you do it? For a good shot at $1,000 or so, I certainly hope you would. In fact, you would probably do that for all potential buyers who are qualified to buy a home, if they asked you.

So why not do it anyway? Suggest to the buyers that reading a completed purchase agreement word for word—after it has been completed with the proper information—would be the wisest move they could make. It would show them exactly where the situation stands.

Talk about attitude boosting! This is good for the buyers, because it shows them every dotted "i" and crossed "t" in the agreement. And it's good for you because it puts you even closer to a sale.

You must be presumptive. Take the lead. Many agents won't fill out the purchase agreement until the buyer actually agrees to buy the home. But that's not working smart, because this completed form can be a powerful sales tool.

REASSURE THE BUYER

How is the buyer going to feel while you're filling out the purchase agreement? Nervous? Yes. Intimidated? Yes. It's probably causing him more stress than the barrel of a loaded cannon pointed at his left ear.

Put the buyer at ease by assuring that the agreement is just for informational purposes only, unless or until the buyer decides to purchase. Repeat again that you are filling it out only to provide the buyer with a copy of all terms and details, so the buyer may make a rational decision. Stress that you don't mind doing it, no matter what the final outcome is, because all you want is for the buyer to make a rational decision.

And when you think about it, that's really what you want. If the buyer already has taken the time to come to your office to be qualified and be questioned in regard to wants, needs, likes and dislikes and has been shown a suitable home, it would be irrational not to buy, right?

That's right. And if the buyer does not want the home, there is nothing you can do to force a purchase short of producing your pistol (and such a sale would never hold up in court!)

Give the buyer something to do while you're filling out the agreement (if you haven't done it already). Perhaps you will need additional information, such as the buyer's credit references. Give the buyers a form to complete to keep them busy while you are handling the purchase agreement. Type the agreement, if you are proficient with a typewriter. It's visually more appealing than handwriting. And in a couple of days, the buyers' attorneys may be looking at it. The more you can impress them, the better off you will be.

DON'T DISCUSS PRICE NOW

If the buyer has never mentioned anything about price, don't ask now if they intend to pay full price. Assume that they will. Treat the purchase agreement as if the buyers already had agreed to full price.

The reason for this is simple. It's the law. When you give a seller a copy of his or her listing, it is, in effect, the same as raising your right hand after placing your left hand on the Bible and swearing that you will do everything in your power to get the price and terms that the seller wants. If you suggest that a buyer might get by with a lower price, you're not living up to your agreement with the seller. And such tactics can rise to haunt you later. Take my word for it. I've seen it happen too many times with too many agents.

Assume the buyer will pay full price for reasons of simplicity. It's easier for you to present a full price offer to a seller than a lower price offer. And you'll get a better commission, also.

And finally, if the buyers don't want to pay full price, they would have told you so by this time. Don't give them any ideas by asking if they want to pay full price.

DEPOSITS

How much deposit do you take on a $90,000 home? Do you know there are some agents who still take $500 or $1,000? That practice is obsolete. It went out when the average price of a house went up from $30,000.

Agents have an obligation to their sellers to get a fair deposit on purchased properties. When preparing the forms, don't list the price or the deposit. Instead, you're going to give your buyer one last chance to leave. Perhaps you can stick your head into the room and say, "By the way, five to ten percent of the sale price is recommended for the deposit. Rather than $9,000, would $4,500 be a little easier for you?"

If the buyer doesn't leave, the worst that could happen, given an alternate choice, is the buyer will select the $4,500 deposit. That still amounts to $3,500 more deposit than most of your competitors would get. Another benefit of higher deposit is it makes your offer more credible. Regardless of the price, a seller is going to be more impressed with an offer with an above-average deposit.

Of course, the buyer may jump up and say, "Wait a minute. I'm not leaving any deposit. I just want to see the papers and get out of here."

If that happens, what do you say? Remember Moneymaker No. 1? That's right, it still works. "No problem," you say. "Remember, this is all just to help you decide."

Your reassurances should calm them again. And now, you're ready for step three, the final step, the move you make to fatten them for the ultimate close: Read the purchase agreement to the buyers. Don't forget the difference between talking and selling is asking questions. Suppose you just read aloud:

> "We, the undersigned, hereby offer and agree to purchase the following land, situated in the city of Warren, Macomb County, Michigan. Described as follows: Commonly being known as 123 Main Street. Together with all improvements, including all lighting fixtures, shades, venetian blinds, curtain rods, storm windows, screens, awnings, TV antenna, and to pay therefore the sum of $94,500, subject to the existing. . . ."

If you merely read, the buyers may tune you out, the same way you did to your high school algebra teacher—the one who talked in monotones.

Ask questions occasionally throughout the reading of the agreement. This will get the buyers to participate. For example:

> "We, the undersigned, hereby offer and agree to purchase the following land, situated in the city of Warren, Macomb County, Michigan. Described as follows. Commonly being known as 123 Main Street. . . . By the way, folks, how does that sound for your new address? . . . Yeah, it does. . . . Together with all improvements, including all lighting fixtures, shades, venetian blinds, curtain rods, storm win-

dows, screens, awnings, TV antenna. . . . You do want the TV antenna, don't you? . . . And to pay therefore the sum of $94,500 subject to the existing. . . ."

Don't just read your purchase agreement. Remember, you're staging a presentation, just like your visual presentation on the listing. And any presentation requires occasional questions. Why? It keeps you in control. It gives you the buyers' attention, and properly asked questions bring agreement, which seems to make it easier for the buyer to make the final agreement.

THE FINAL AGREEMENT

When you've finished reading the purchase agreement, you have done all that you can. There are only two more things to say.

1. Any questions? (Moneymaker No. 3, remember? If they do have questions, answer them. If not, proceed to step number two.)

2. I'll need your okay right here. And press hard, this is cheap carbon. We need to get your signature on all six copies to make sure it's legible on yours.

After you've made that last statement, say no more. Hand the buyers a pen. And wait.

Most of the time (and again, that's good odds in this business), they'll take the pen and sign on the dotted lines. And you will have made a sale. You will have truly earned the commission that you would have lost with your buyers in the parking lot if you hadn't stopped them from leaving. And you did this by staying on the track. You led the buyers toward the point in time when they could make a logical decision.

DECISIONS ARE DIFFICULT

There is something strange about making decisions. People tend to shy away from them. They like to stay in their comfort zones of blissful indecision. "Nothing ventured, nothing lost" is the way many people look at making any kind of move that might be to their benefit. Making decisions is not easy, so people often decide not to decide.

Talk about something that hurts! Living your whole life not making any decisions can be frustrating indeed, especially in retrospect. It's easy not to decide now, but when a person looks over life after most of it already has been spent, it's easy to ask, "Why didn't I ever do that?" And "that" could be anything from getting a better job to moving into a new residence.

But prospects often are indecisive. And you have a certain obligation to close on them, to help them get out of that comfort zone of indecision. After all, if they didn't want to leave it, they never would have come to your office for the qualification visit.

So the best place to close on a buyer is in your office. That's where all your tools you need to cope with any objection the buyers may raise are located. Any other place is good. Some places are better than others, but even the worst is good.

Close on the buyer anywhere you believe you can get a signed purchase agreement. Close in the lounge of a local restaurant, close inside of a car, close on the fender if they can't wait.

Second to the office, the best place to close on buyers is at the home you've just shown them, provided the situation is right and no one is at home.

SELLING ISN'T SO BAD

Wouldn't it be nice if we didn't have to sell so hard? Wouldn't it be nice if sellers would call and say, "Please come list my house, I'm ready to sell?" Wouldn't it be nice, also, if buyers would call us and say, "I'm ready to buy a house. May I please come into your office to be qualified, and would you carefully select three properties from which I can choose, so I can buy with the least delay possible?"

Why can't it be that way? People buy and sell homes every day. Why do people need to be "sold"?

It doesn't matter why. That's just the way it is. Multi-million-dollar producers don't mind selling. They do it lots of times.

And I hope you will, too.

IN A CAPSULE

1. Buyers are nervous people, and for good reason. They are considering multi-thousand-dollar investments. Don't lose them after showing them "the right house." Get them into the office either by offering to answer more questions, to fill out all forms so the buyer can make a rational decision or to sell the house at $10,000 less than the listed price. You may not be able to do it, but you can at least get the buyer into the office.

2. During the basic closing, discuss and iron out details with the buyer. Also, recap the buyer's down payment and financial monthly installment.

3. If a buyer hasn't mentioned paying less than asking price, assume the buyer intends to pay full price. Don't give the buyer any ideas by asking if he or she intends to pay full price. Assume it. If the buyer didn't want to pay full price, you would have been informed before closing.

4. The practice of collecting $1,000 deposits on homes went out years ago. Deposits today range from five to ten percent. An agent's responsibility is to get a healthy deposit on a home. And a good deposit makes a good impression on a seller.

5. After reading the purchase agreement to the buyer, ask if the buyer has any questions. If so, answer them. If not, hand the buyer a pen, ask for a signature, then wait. And be quiet. Don't talk yourself out of a sale.

List the most important points you have gained from the
preceding Strategy:

_____

_____

_____

_____

_____

_____

_____

_____

_____

_____

_____

_____

_____

_____

_____

_____

NOTES

Epilogue

Now that you've finished reading this book, I hope that you will be able to take the principles offered in it with you to the real world. But just because you've read the book once doesn't mean that you have learned the principles.

Remember: Practice, drill and rehearse. That's the only way you can ever learn anything well enough to push it into your subconscious mind. And that's where you want all of these principles to be stored for future reference.

To get anywhere in the real estate business, you have to believe in it. That doesn't mean you have to work twelve-hour days, six and seven days a week. But when you do work, you have to know what you're doing. And you have to be good at it, because you have a lot of competition.

It's often been said that from the moment a person gets into the real estate business, he or she is fighting the odds to stay in. And that's probably true, considering the high dropout rate.

You can stay in the business, if you learn to work smart, and I hope this book will help you do that.

And so, as we close, let me leave you with a five-point formula to assure your success in the real estate business.

1. *Starting tomorrow, work on bringing in salable listings.* The amount of money you make in real estate will be in direct proportion to the number of listings with your name on them.

2. *Separate lookers from buyers.* If anything will kill you in this business, it's wasting all your waking hours on lookers. Remember, seek not the living among the dead.

3. *Show homes to qualified buyers only.* Don't show $100,000 homes to $70,000 customers. It's a waste of time. Everyone would love to buy the nicer home, but find out which customers are able to buy the nicer homes, and show those to them.

4. *Show in-house listings to your customers.* You'll close a higher percentage of them if you show them regularly. And the more in-house listings you show, the better off financially you will be.

5. *Invest in real estate.* Remember what Gerald O'Hara said in *Gone With the Wind,* "Land is the only thing worth living for, worth fighting for, worth dying for, because land is the only thing that lasts." And since no more of it is being made, it's value should steadily increase.

Best of luck to you, and remember: An agent won't make real money in this business until he or she is willing to persist beyond that first rejection. Shoot for the moon, and you'll fall among the stars.

For Further Information

For information on Floyd's availability to speak at your next seminar, rally, or convention, or for questions regarding this book and other Floyd Wickman products, write Floyd Wickman and Associates, 2119 East Fourteen Mile Road, Sterling Heights, Michigan 48310 or call (313) 978–1900.